In Memory of John and Alice Peterson

John Peterson
Mind, Truth and Teleology
An Introduction to Scholastic Philosophy

editiones scholasticae
Volume 49

John Peterson

Mind, Truth and Teleology

An Introduction to Scholastic Philosophy

editiones scholasticae

Bibliographic information published by Deutsche Nationalbibliothek
The Deutsche Nationalbibliothek lists this publication in the Deutsche Nationalbibliographie;
detailed bibliographic data is available in the Internet at http://dnb.ddb.de

Distribution:

North and South America by
Transaction Books
Rutgers University
Piscataway, NJ 08854-8042
trans@transactionpub.com

United Kingdom, Ireland, Iceland, Turkey, Malta, Portugal by
Gazelle Books Services Limited
White Cross Mills
Hightown
LANCASTER, LA1 4XS
sales@gazellebooks.co.uk

©2015 editiones scholasticae
Postfach 15 41, D-63133 Heusenstamm
www.editiones-scholasticae.de

ISBN 978-3-86838-555-7

2015

No part of this book may be reproduced, stored in retrieval systems or transmitted
in any form or by any means, electronic, mechanical, photocopying, microfilming, recording or otherwise
without written permission from the Publisher, with the exception of any material supplied specifically for the
purpose of being entered and executed on a computer system, for exclusive use of the purchaser of the work.

Printed on acid-free paper

Printed in Germany
by Strauss GmbH

Table of Contents

1.	Are There Final Causes?	1
2.	Truth and Teleology	12
3.	Are We Drawn to the Truth?	26
4.	The Bearer of Truth	45
5.	True Belief and Knowledge Revisited	52
6.	Mind and the Problem of Realism	61
7.	Logic and the Mind–Body Problem	77
8.	The Paradox of the Soul	91
9.	Dialectical Mind	105

Chapter One
Are There Final Causes?

Construing efficient causes as beginning and ending with their effects spawns the dilemma that a given effect or event either always occurs or never occurs.[1] One escapes the dilemma by distinguishing basic and subsidiary efficient causes, according temporal priority of causes to their effects in the case of the former. In the case of human making and doing, where the two efficient causes belong to the same subject, the two are supplemented by a final cause which serves to link or to mediate them. This it does by drawing out or actuating the subsidiary cause which exists potentially in the basic cause. Arguing from analogy, one can show that, just when basic and subsidiary efficient causes belong to the same non-human subject in nature, they must likewise be supplemented by final causes if the potentiality of subsidiary causes in basic causes is to be drawn out and made actual.

The first step in all this is to spell out the dilemma in question. The second is to show how by distinguishing basic and subsidiary efficient causes and according temporal priority to the former one escapes the dilemma. It will be found that these two causes in some cases need to be linked, and this requires a cause of a different type, a final cause. However, toward these ends some distinctions must first be made.

Efficient causes are either actual or potential, proper or incidental.[2] That makes four possibilities: (1) actual, proper efficient causes, (2) potential, proper efficient causes, (3) actual, incidental efficient causes, and (4) potential, incidental efficient causes. As for (1), Phidias sculpturing is the actual efficient cause of the coming-to-be of *Athena*. As for (2), Phidias as sculptor, i.e. as having the art of sculpture, is the potential proper efficient cause of *Athena*'s coming to be. As for (3), just in case Phidias is musical, a musical person

---

[1] Much of this chapter originally appeared in *Proceedings of the American Catholic Philosophical Association*, vol. 78, 2004, 161-167.

[2] See Aristotle, *Physics*, Book II, ch. 3, 195a-195b, 3 in *The Basic Works of Aristotle*, edited by Richard McKeon, New York, 1941.

sculpturing is the actual, if incidental, efficient cause of *Athena's* coming-to-be. Since it is incidental to a sculptor sculpturing that he is musical, one says in a manner of speaking that when a musical sculptor sculptures, musical sculptures. So one says that when Phidias, who happens to be musical, sculptures, musical person sculpturing is the cause of the coming-to-be of *Athena*. But it is incidentally and not properly the actual efficient cause of that effect. And as for (4), just in case, once again, Phidias is musical, musical sculptor is the potential, incidental cause of *Athena's* coming-to-be. Since it is once again incidental to a person as having the art of sculpture (i.e. as sculptor) that he or she is musical, one says that when Phidias sculptures *Athena*, musical sculptor is the cause of *Athena's* coming-to-be. But it is incidentally and not properly the potential efficient cause of that effect.

When they are persons, both actual and potential proper efficient causes have ends. They tend toward something else which completes and fulfills them. But the ends are different in each case. The end of Phidias sculpturing is a certain *objet d'art*, i.e. *Athena*. But the end of Phidias as having the art of sculpture (i.e. as sculptor) is sculpturing. Further, when Phidias sculptures *Athena*, Phidias' sculpturing begins and ceases with *Athena's* being sculptured. And musical person sculpturing is likewise simultaneous with *Athena's* being sculptured.

This simultaneity sparks the dilemma of efficient causes. Take Phidias sculpturing *Athena* and call this S. S either begins to be or not. If not, then Phidias always sculptures *Athena* and *Athena* is always being sculptured. But that is false. The sculpturing of *Athena* has a beginning in time. But if S *does* begin to be, then its beginning to be must be caused by something else, S1. To cause S, S1 must be an actual and not a mere potential cause. If S1 is also an acting efficient cause, then like S, S1 is a complex of a thing as acting or operating and is simultaneous with its effect, S. S is Phidias' beginning to sculpture and the supposed cause, S1, is something moving Phidias in that action. S1 is thus the logically prior actual efficient cause in this case.

S1 for its part either begins to be or not. If not, then, acting causes and their effects being simultaneous, then once again Phidias always sculptures *Athena* and *Athena* is always being sculptured. But if S1 *does* begin to be through a further acting efficient cause, S2, then cause and effect are again simultaneous. As for S2, it must either begin to be or not. And once again the answer can only be that it does begin to be. Otherwise, acting efficient causes and their effects being simultaneous, it must again be countenanced that Phidias always sculptures *Athena*. But if S2 does begin to be, then it must be caused by still another acting efficient cause, S3, and so on, *ad infinitum*. And then, since each cause causes only because it is simultaneously caused by another, there is no sufficient reason for Phidias' sculpturing *Athena*. Phidias, then, *never* sculptures *Athena*. If S1 causes S only because S1 is at the same time caused by S2, and if S2 causes S1 only because it is at the same time caused by S3, and so on to infinity, then there is no first efficient cause and hence no other cause. S, then, does not occur. Nor does it help to posit an absolute first actual efficient cause, S_n, in this chain. If only active efficient causes are admitted, then, if S_n has no cause, then S_n always is. But then the first horn of the dilemma takes hold again and Phidias always sculptures *Athena*.

The same dilemma threatens efficient causation in nature as well. Suppose that a paramecium, say, *a*, begins to split, the consequence of which is a new paramecium, *b*. *a*'s splitting (call it P) is the acting efficient cause of the effect, i.e. *b*'s coming-to-be. Now either P begins to be or not. If not, then *b* is always emerging. If so, and all causes are acting efficient causes, then some other efficient cause, P1, is causing *a* to split. But for its part, P1 either begins to be or not. If not, then, since P1 always occurs and is simultaneous with P, it follows once again that P has no beginning. Appearances to the contrary, *a* is always splitting. But if P1 *does* begin to be, then a still prior efficient cause, P2, is required to cause P1 to begin to be, and so on, *ad infinitum*. And then, since each cause causes only because it is being caused by another, and so on without end, there is no sufficient reason for P. But then neither P nor its effect, the birth of *b*, occurs. Nor as before does it avail to posit an absolute first acting efficient cause in the chain, say P_n. If only active efficient causes are allowed, then, if P_n is uncaused, then P_n always is. But then the first horn of the dilemma again looms large and *a* is always splitting. If, therefore, one restricts causes to active efficient causes, then the same dilemma breaks out. Either the event P always occurs or else it never occurs. *a* either always splits or never splits. In art and nature both, therefore, the same dilemma stands. How is it escaped?

Since the dilemma surfaces only because it is assumed that efficient causes and their effects begin and cease together, one escapes the dilemma by surrendering that assumption and assuming instead that such causes precede their effects. Take P which is *a* birthing *b*. Since P evidently begins to be, P is caused by a preceding efficient cause, P1. P1, say, is the maturing of *a* which triggers *a*'s birthing *b*. P1 in turn, is caused by another cause, P2, which is temporally prior to P1, and so on. Note that in this temporal causal chain, no one cause causes its effect only because it is *simultaneously* caused to do so by another.

This reply is right about what occasions the dilemma. For the dilemma surfaces only if it is essential and not accidental to the causal action of any cause *c* with respect to its effect *e* that *c* is caused by another. Recall our example. If P begins to be by P1 and P1 begins to be by P2, and so on, where all causes cause only because they are simultaneously caused by another, then either P *always* is, just in case there is a first cause P*n*, or else P *never* is, just in case there is no first cause. But if one drops the assumption of simultaneity, then the fork collapses. If the various causes in the chain do not begin and cease together, then it no longer follows that the effect at hand is either always occurring or that it never occurs. The dilemma in question is thus broken.

Since dropping the assumption of simultaneity sidesteps the dilemma, one must see if that assumption is relinquished without reducing actual efficient causes to mere potential efficient causes. For potential efficient causes such as Phidias as sculptor always precede actual effects and yet are clearly insufficient for those effects. So the question is, can efficient causes temporally precede their effects and yet be sufficient for those effects without admitting final causes? If so, then our dilemma is bypassed and effects explained to boot.

In some cases this seems possible. Suppose a wind-gust hurls a stick against my windshield, breaking the wiper-blade. One plausibly says that the gust is the basic cause and the impacting stick the subsidiary cause of the break. The stick, after all, impacts the blade only because it is driven by the preceding gust. In any case, it seems that here basic and subsidiary causes are together sufficient for the effect without admitting final causes, and entities should not be unnecessarily multiplied. If that is so and if the basic efficient cause here temporally precedes both the subsidiary cause and the effect, it seems that our dilemma of efficient causes is avoided and the effect in question explained.

Yet in our two examples, basic and subsidiary efficient causes are not jointly sufficient for the effect without admitting final causes. The reason for this is that, while time separates them as it does the wind-gust and the stick, they are not, like the latter, unrelated. In the case of Phidias, let us identify the basic cause with Phidias' choice of *Athena* and the subsidiary cause with his sculpturing. Since the former precedes the latter, our dilemma is bypassed. Moreover, since Phidias as choosing *Athena* is prone to cutting it, the two are not foreign to each other. The one lies coiled in the other. And since choice implies an end, a final cause causally contributes to the effect. It is identified with Phidias' ideal pattern or model of *Athena* for the sake of which he carves. The final cause thus pre-exists in and elicits action from the agent.

In this analysis one distinguishes four causal contributors. The first is the form of *Athena* in Phidias' mind considered simply as form. It is perhaps one of many models contemplated by Phidias. The second is his choosing to replicate that form in stone. On the heels of that choice, the third is that same form considered as end. And the fourth, elicited by that end, is Phidias' sculpturing. Note that the basic and subsidiary efficient causes are here linked by the final cause. Note too the reciprocity between the basic efficient cause and the formal cause. The form of *Athena* in Phidias is the condition of his choice. One chooses or picks out only what one knows and knowledge is of form. Yet his choice of *Athena* is the condition of the latter's becoming an end.

This same analysis holds for a's splitting. Activities like this match human actions in that cause and effect begin and cease to be together. a taken as birthing b begins and ceases with b's being birthed, just as Phidias' cutting *Athena* begins and ceases with *Athena*'s being cut. Yet we saw that if all causes are efficient causes and begin and cease together, then effects either always occur or never occur. To break this, we need only say that some basic efficient cause moves a to split but once again insist that this cause *precedes* the event instead of beginning and ceasing with the event. Let us identify this basic efficient cause with a's maturing which makes it prone to split. So far three of our previous four causal contributors obtain. First there is the form of paramecium in a from which its maturing processes issue. This corresponds to the form of *Athena* in Phidias which conditions his choice of *Athena*. Second, there are the maturing processes themselves. This corresponds to Phidias' choice to sculpture *Athena*. Third, there is the subsidiary efficient cause, a's splitting, which corresponds to Phidias' sculpturing. Yet right here some say the parallelism ends. For since there is no question of a's choosing to split, why admit a final cause in this case? Why not say that a's maturing processes are sufficient for its splitting without recourse to a final cause?

The answer harks back to the contrast between basic and subsidiary causes here and in the case of the wind-gust and the stick. We saw that the latter two causes are unrelated while the former are so related that the one lies coiled in the other. a's maturing potentially includes its splitting no less than Phidias' choosing *Athena* potentially includes his sculpturing it. But just for that reason is something needed to actuate the potential. Something must actualize a's potential to split once its maturing processes create that potential. That cannot be something of the same kind, i.e. a third *efficient* cause, basic or subsidiary, standing as between the other two. Otherwise the question of linkage only recurs. A fourth such cause is needed to tie the third to either one of the original two, inviting a Bradleian *progressus* to infinity. And then a never splits. It is the same with Phidias. Something must actualize his cutting of *Athena*, which lies coiled in his choice of *Athena*. That is not a third efficient cause linking his choice to his sculpturing. Otherwise a fourth is needed to tie *that* cause to his sculpturing, and so on *ad infinitum*. And then Phidias never sculptures. So linking the two causes and actuating the potential require a cause of a different ontological kind. This final cause is no event like the things it ties but the form of *Athena* in Phidias' mind which attracts *a fronte* Phidias' sculpturing of *Athena*. Just so and for the same reason must a cause of a different kind tie or mediate basic and subsidiary efficient causes in the case of a. That cause can only be the form or essence of paramecium in a considered as end or final cause of a's splitting.

Here is how the linkage works in both cases. The effect is in both cases an event, i.e. *Athena*'s coming-to-be and b's coming-to-be, respectively. The two efficient causes in the first are Phidias choosing *Athena* as his model and his actual cutting of it, whereas the two efficient causes in the second case are a's maturing processes and a's splitting. In the first case what links the two is the form of *Athena* in Phidias which, once chosen, becomes the goal of his cutting. This serves as mediator, linking basic and subsidiary causes, because it is behind them both and internal to the agent. Before Phidias chooses *Athena*, the latter is just an idea in his mind, lacking attractive force. But no sooner does he choose *Athena* than that same idea becomes a magnet, drawing out of him the activity of cutting. Note that the self-same form of *Athena* is behind both his choice and his cutting. You only choose and sculpture what you know. Thus do four causal contributors occur successively, forming a difference in unity. The formal cause conditions the basic efficient cause which brings on the mediating final cause, which finally elicits the subsidiary efficient cause.

The same pattern holds for a's birthing b. The form of a is the condition of its maturing processes. Yet those processes are what make that form the end of its splitting. Thus are formal and efficient causes reciprocal. No sooner do those maturing processes, which we have identified with the basic efficient cause, occur in a than the form of paramecium in a assumes attractiveness, drawing out of a the activity of splitting. Recall that no sooner does Phidias select *Athena* than that mental model becomes a magnet, drawing out of him the activity of sculpturing. As the form of *Athena* pre-exists intelligibly in Phidias, so too does the form of b pre-exist naturally in a.[3] Note that the basic efficient causes in both cases, i.e. a's maturing and Phidias' choosing *Athena*, confer on the pre-existing form the status of end or final cause. As the form of *Athena* in Phidias becomes the end of his cutting once he chooses *Athena*, so too does the form of paramecium in a become the end of a's splitting once a's maturity is effected. When in each case the basic efficient cause obtains, the form which already pre-exists in the agent becomes an end, drawing or eliciting from the agent activity that is means to that end. Thus is that form a final cause, linking or mediating the two other causes. And the result of all four causes is in each case the reproduction of that same pre-existing form.

The two efficient causes in both cases are a difference in unity. Not only is each cause part of the same substance, i.e. Phidias and a,

---

[3] See St. Thomas Aquinas, *Summa theologiae*, I, Q.15, a.1 in *Introduction to St. Thomas Aquinas*, edited by A. Pegis, New York, 1948, p.162.

respectively, but also each one springs from the same source within that substance, i.e. the form of *Athena* in Phidias and the form of paramecium in *a*, respectively. Moreover, the shared form in each case assumes the status of end. Phidias as choosing *Athena* tends to the form of *Athena* within him, and *a* as maturing tends to the form of paramecium within it. Without espousing Hegelianism, one can say that here unity lurks behind the difference of the two causes, whereas in the foregoing case of the wind-gust and the stick all there is is brute difference. The gust and the stick are neither parts of the same subject nor do they spring from the same form within that subject. Since no common subject stands behind the two, there is no question of one's causing a bent in that subject toward the other or toward the form of that subject. Finally, since they are unrelated and one is not in the first instance potentially in the other, there is no need of a final cause to actuate that potential.

To sum it up, if all causes are efficient causes which begin and cease with their effects, then any event either always occurs or else never occurs. But either alternative flouts our experience. The fact is that Phidias begins to sculpture *Athena* and *a* begins to birth *b*. To cover this and save efficient causes from the jaws of the dilemma, one distinguishes basic and subsidiary efficient causes, according temporal priority to the former. But just when, as in cases like these, both causes belong to the same subject and are conditioned by the same form within that subject, the one includes the other as a live possibility. Here is where final causes come into play. For some third cause must actuate that possibility and that third cause is neither a cause nor a being in the same sense in which the causes it links are causes and beings. Otherwise the live possibility or potentiality goes unrealized and the gap is never bridged.

In all of this, the order of conditions runs as follows. The form both conditions and is conditioned by the basic efficient cause. The former is the source of the latter while the latter gives the former the status of end or goal. As end or goal of the subsidiary efficient cause, the form is the condition of that cause which in turn is the condition of the effect.

So it is that there is a double reciprocity. While basic efficient causes make forms into ends to begin with, subsidiary efficient causes realize those ends in matter. And while subsidiary efficient causes cause the realization of final causes in matter, final causes for their part initiate that causality. Exercising makes for fitness, says Aristotle, but fitness makes for exercising.[4] He might have said instead that sculpturing makes for *Athena*, but that *Athena* makes for sculpturing, or that splitting makes for paramecium, but that paramecium makes for splitting. And finally, all four causal contributors, i.e. formal, basic efficient, final, and subsidiary efficient are, along with matter, sufficient conditions of the effect.

Nevertheless, an objection to finalism takes the form of a dilemma. For either the end pre-exists the bent toward it or not. If not, then it cannot instigate that bent. If so, then since it already is, it is nonsense to say that something moves toward it.

For example, suppose that paramecium *a* begins the reproductive process of binary fission. Either the supposed end of *a*'s splitting, the offspring paramecium *b*, already exists or not. If so, then it is nonsense to say that *a*'s splitting is tending toward *b* since *b* already is. If not, then it is impossible in the first place for *b* to elicit *a*'s reproductive process of *a* toward it. What does not exist cannot elicit anything. The same dilemma threatens Aristotle's example. For suppose that formal, efficient and final causes are one in species in the case of man producing man.[5] Then we can once again ask whether the final cause pre-exists the effect or not. If so, then since the final cause (i.e. the species man) already is, it is senseless to say that the change in question is tending toward it. But if not, then it can hardly elicit the movement of the efficient cause toward it.

A possible answer distinguishes individual and nature. Under it, *a* tends toward its own nature, the nature of paramecium. Since that nature already exists in *a*, there is then no problem about how it elicits the movement of *a* toward it. Thus one sidesteps the second horn of the dilemma. But since that nature does not already exist *as exemplified in b*, then neither is it problematic to say that *a* is moving toward it, thus disarming the first horn of the dilemma. In other words, this escape recognizes that *b* both already is and is not, though in different respects. As paramecium, *b* already is but as *this* paramecium that is false. So the solution invokes the distinction between individual and nature.

[4] Aristotle, *Physics*, Bk II, ch. 3. (195a, 9-10).
[5] Aristotle, *Physics*, trans. R.P. Hardie and R.K.Gaye, in R. McKeon, ed., *The Basic Works of Aristotle* (New York: Random House, 1941), Book II, 7 (198a 26), 248.

Yet this escape is more apparent than real. For either the goal of a's splitting is the nature of paramecium or the individual paramecium b. If the former, then since that nature is already exemplified in a, then it is nonsense to say that a or for that matter anything else aims to realize it. But if the latter, then since b evidently does not already exist, then how can it influence the movement of a or for that matter anything else toward it? But this it must do to be the end of a's movement.

Nevertheless, a modification of this might serve to bypass the fork. For one can say that the end of a's splitting is the nature or species of paramecium and that this does pre-exist a's splitting, since a does exemplify that species. However, this does not imply the ogre that a's splitting is moving toward the realization of that nature, even though the latter already exists in a. For what a's splitting aims at is the nature of paramecium as realized in the effect b, whereas what pre-exists in a is the nature of paramecium taken as goal or plan.[6] So by distinguishing nature as goal and nature as effect of a goal, one skirts the dilemma of ends. In terms of Aristotle's four causes, this is to distinguish the final and formal cause in any change.

Nevertheless, this answer fails in other alleged cases of natural ends such as growth or maturation. Thus, either the form of a mature frog pre-exists in the tadpole as goal of the latter's bent toward it or not. If so, then since that end already exists, it is contradictory to say that the tadpole tends towards it. But if not, then that form cannot draw the tadpole's movement toward it. Unlike reproduction as in the case of the paramecium, the answer here cannot be that the mature frog post-exists the tadpole's movement toward it as effect or formal cause, whereas its likeness pre-exists in the tadpole as goal or final cause. For the supposed end, the mature frog, evidently does not actually exist in the tadpole. So the dilemma of ends still stands for alleged natural ends in which the mature form of an organism is said to be the end or goal of developmental changes in an immature form of that organism. In such cases, one must either deny that the adult form of the maturing organism is the natural goal of the pro-

---

[6] Aquinas seems to adopt this pattern. *See Summa contra gentiles*, trans. A. Pegis in *Introduction to St. Thomas Aquinas* (New York: The Modern Library, 1948), Book III, Ch. II, 431.

cess or else succumb to the dilemma of ends. To use a stock example, either the oak pre-exists the bent of the acorn toward it or not. If not, then it can hardly instigate that bent. If so, then since it already actually is, it cannot be said that the acorn is moving toward it. Nothing tends toward what it already is.

It might seem that an Aristotelian answer to this avails. It is that the oak both pre-exists the acorn's bent toward it and does not pre-exist the acorn's bent toward it but in different respects. To the extent that it does not *actually* pre-exist the acorn's bent toward it, it can meaningfully be said that the acorn tends toward it. What does not already actually exist can be tended toward. But to the extent that the oak at least *potentially* pre-exists the acorn's bent toward it and potential existence is not simple non-existence, then the (potential) oak can instigate the acorn's movement toward being an (actual) oak. Yet the evident counter-reply here is that nothing that is only potentially the case can instigate anything actual. It takes something actual to do that, whether the cause in question is final or efficient. Phidias' mere potential end to cut the *Athena* cannot induce him begin cutting it, nor can his state of merely potentially cutting the *Athena* cause it to begin to be cut.

A possible clue to escaping the fork comes from human purpose. Here, the end does pre-exist the bent toward it. Thus the *Athena* pre-exists in Phidias' mind as mental model. Yet one cannot say that because it does it is nonsense to say that Phidias is moving toward that end. That would hold only if the end already exists *in re* whereas it only already exists *in mente*. Similarly, one might hypothesize that natural ends pre-exist in God's mind as final causes of natural changes. Many would doubtless prefer to drop natural ends than to admit this way out of the dilemma. Yet one cannot *a priori* rule out an independent argument for divine Ideas as ends, and such an argument is proffered in Chapter Three.

Chapter Two
Truth and Teleology

The preceding chapter made a case for teleology in things. The present chapter argues for teleology in truth. Though we ordinarily distinguish theoretical and practical truth, it is seldom noted that the latter can be a condition of the former. That means that practical truth is not wholly derivative of theoretical truth. So defining truth as the conformity of thought to thing is too narrow to catch practical truth which is the conformity of thing to thought. From the viewpoint of truth's being the sharing of some pattern as between mind and thing, the definition of truth as the conformity of thought *and* thing is more adequate since it covers both theoretical and practical truth.

Artists call their works true not because they elicit true judgments but because they conform to their ideal models as ends. Thus in, "This is the true production" practical truth conditions and is not conditioned by propositional truth. That is our cue that teleology figures in the agreement of thought and thing, the genus of truth. It is just that in practical truth the ideal is (generally) the end of the real while in theoretical truth the real is the end of the ideal.

The two truths also differ in their relation to theoretical and practical knowledge, respectively. Artists know their models even before artifacts conform to them. So here there can be knowledge without truth. Yet there is no practical truth without the corresponding knowledge. By contrast, theoretical truth does not imply knowledge-*that*, but knowledge-*that does* imply theoretical truth. Finally as within theoretical truth, truth and knowledge are related such that though the truth of P implies neither one's knowledge that-P nor the meta-knowledge of P's truth, i.e. of P's conformity to reality, one's knowledge that-P both implies and is implied by P's truth plus the meta-knowledge of P's truth or of P's conformity to reality.

I

To bring all this out, one might begin with the following question: Is practical truth or the truth of making and doing derivative of theoretical or propositional truth? Things, artifacts, events, actions, etc. are called practically true when they measure up or conform to their ideal patterns. Thus, we call art works true when they match their mental models, speech true when it maps a speaker's belief, and a missile's course true when it follows its planned flight path. Medieval realists call natural things true because they conform to their archetypes in God's mind, and so on. And the question is whether these senses of 'true' feed off the propositional sense of 'true'. Are the things just mentioned called true only elliptically, i.e. only because a true proposition can be made about them or is that not the case? Is a sculpture called true only because one can truly say of it, "This copies the sculptor's model" (hereafter, the one-truth theory) or is the sense of 'true' here independent of propositional truth (hereafter, the two-truth theory)? It is here argued that the latter is true and hence that truth divides into two kinds, theoretical and practical. Yet a single thread ties the two or else nothing common binds 'true judgment' and 'true production,' and something does. Judgments are true when they map the real while art works are true when they match the ideal. What they share is the conformity of mind and thing.[7] Yet this is unacceptably vague. For in what does this conformity consist? When mind agrees with thing or thing with mind how is this agreement to be understood?

Next, theoretical and practical truth are contrasted as to their relation to theoretical and practical knowledge respectively. Here the relation of the truth of theory to theoretical knowledge is just the opposite of that between the truth of practice and practical knowledge. Third and last, as within theoretical truth it is proposed that though the truth of a proposition P implies neither one's knowledge that-P nor one's acquaintance with P's truth, one's knowledge that-P both implies and is implied by P's truth coupled with one's acquaintance with P's truth.

---

[7] The *differentia* is that in true judgments mind always conforms to thing while in works of art thing generally conforms to mind.

II

According to the two-truth theory which Aquinas and other medieval thinkers espoused, truth adds nothing real to being since outside of being is nothing at all. Yet since 'truth' expresses something that 'being' does not, truth adds conceptually to being. It adds to being a certain way or mode, namely being as assimilated to mind. From the standpoint of what it adds to being, truth is defined as being as assimilated to mind either as measure of being or as measured by being. As assimilated to mind as a measure of being, truth is either in God's mind as divine Exemplar of creatures or in our minds as the exemplar of artifacts. This is the truth of things or practical truth which is primarily in God's mind and secondarily in our minds. As assimilated to mind as something measured, truth is in our minds as concepts or judgments. This is theoretical truth which, since God is in no sense measured, is in our minds only. As to the latter, when we know what a condor is, being in the sense of essence or "whatness" takes on a mental mode and that is the mode of a concept. In things the mode of condor is particular and concrete but as a concept in mind it is universal and abstract. To the extent that it takes on the latter aspect in mind being acquires the aspect of truth or the assimilation of being to mind. Further, when we affirm "Some condors are birds that nest in the Andes Mountains", being in the sense of fact once again takes on a mental mode but this time it is the mode of judgment. In reality, the constituents of facts are not separate but always united. Nesting in the Andes Mountains is not something abstracted from the condors that do that. Yet in recording that fact in the foregoing judgment, we both abstract that feature *via* the predicate from those condors taken as subject and unite it to the subject *via* the copula 'are'. Thus, to the extent that being is received in mind according to mind's own mode of composing and dividing in judgment, being once again acquires the aspect of truth or the assimilation to mind.[8]

And yet, being takes on the aspect of truth more properly in judgment than in the simple apprehension of essences. Nothing be-

---

[8] This accords with Aquinas' general dictum that the received is in the receiver according to the mode of the receiver. Hence, being is in mind according to the mode of mind. See St. Thomas Aquinas, *Summa theologica* I, q 84, a 1.

comes conformed to itself but as a dyadic relation conformity requires distinct terms. Hence, truth is in mind when mind adds something of its own which is not in things but which nonetheless expresses the conformity of mind and thing.[9] This fails to occur in simple apprehension where mind only passively receives essences without adding any act or relation of its own.[10] It instead takes place in mind's act of composing and dividing subject and predicate. When mind judges that the thing apprehended *via* the subject conforms to its idea of it in the predicate then mind adds something of its own, i.e. the relation of subject and predicate. In other words, since truth is the conformity of mind and thing and since mind expresses this only through its own device of composing and dividing subject and predicate, then truth is properly found only in judgments and just in those judgments that do conform to things.[11] Ordinary language reflects this since no one predicates 'true' of words or concepts such as the word or concept 'condor', but only of judgments as when we affirm that some condors nest in the Andes Mountains.

Thus is truth the conformity of mind and thing.[12] It is primarily in mind and secondarily in things.[13] Alternatively, it is the agreement of something, whether mind or thing, to its source.[14] In theoretical truth reality as source or ground measures mind as when facts make our judgments true. And here mind agrees with its source. But in

---

[9] St. Thomas Aquinas, *De veritate* trans. by Robert Mulligan, S.J. (Chicago: Henry Regnery, 1952) vol. I, q 1 a 3, 13.

[10] St. Thomas Aquinas, *De veritate* trans. by Robert Mulligan, S.J. (Chicago: Henry Regnery, 1952) vol. I, q 1 a 3, 13.

[11] By 'truth' here it is meant theoretical and not practical truth. The latter also consists in the conformity of mind and thing but here the bearer of truth is not judgment but ideas, either God's or ours. By 'truth' here is also meant secondary truth since our true judgments do not measure but are measured by things.

[12] St. Thomas Aquinas, *De veritate* trans. Robert Mulligan, S.J. (Chicago: Henry Regnery, 1952) vol. I, q I, a1, 6.

[13] St. Thomas Aquinas, *De veritate* trans. by Robert Mulligan, S.J., vol. I, q 1, a 2, 11.

[14] St. Thomas Aquinas, *Summa theologiae* trans.by Thomas Gilby, O.P. (London: Blackfriars, in conjunction with Eyre & Spottiswoode, 1964) I a q 16, a1, vol. IV, 76-79. In theoretical truth the source to which mind corresponds is the real or non-mental. In practical truth the source to which things correspond (and in which truth properly speaking resides) is mind.

practical truth it works the other way around. Mind as source or ground measures things as when artists' ideal models measure their artifacts. Yet either agreement requires the conformity or union of thing and mind. Artifacts are true just when they match or are one with their mental models. However, this union or equation can only occur in a mind.[15] It is not any natural thing or artifact that takes on the forms of other things while remaining what it is. It is a mind that does that.[16] Thus, Phidias' mind takes on various forms which he contemplates reproducing in stone including the form of *Athena*. And the point is that in order to serve as models or exemplary causes of the artifacts that are made after them, these forms must be present in mind. To be so they must conform to the mode of mind. Thus, to carve *Athena* which as artifact is in marble, the form of *Athena* as mental model must not be in marble or any other stone. It must have psychological and not real being. It is the same in theoretical truth. Our minds take on the forms of various things in knowing them. But once again in order to enter our minds those forms must conform to the way or mode of intellect. Thus in the fact itself of *Athena's* being made of marble the property of being made of marble is not separated from that statue. Yet in order to register that fact in my judgment, "The *Athena* is made of marble" one mentally sets off predicate from subject as a condition of uniting them by the copula 'is'. Again, being canine is always individual in things. There is never just canine but Rex, Lassie, Spot, etc. Yet to know intellectually or define what these individuals are one can only use the mode of mind which is universal. So not only is truth the conformity of mind and thing but this union can only take place in minds and not in things. Thus, being cannot be known unless it conforms to mind or intellect and so cannot be known without the true.[17]

[15] St. Thomas Aquinas, *De veritate* trans. by Robert Mulligan, S.J. vol. I, q I, a 2, 10.

[16] St. Thomas Aquinas, *De veritate* trans. by Robert Mulligan, S.J. vol. I, q 1 a 3, 13; St. Thomas Aquinas, *Commentary on Aristotle's De Anima*, trans. by K. Foster and S. Humphries (New Haven: Yale University Press, 1965) #686, 406-407. See also, Aristotle, *De Anima* in Richard McKeon, ed., *The Basic Works of Aristotle* (New York: Random House, 1941 Bk III, chap. 4 (429a 10-18), 589.

[17] St. Thomas Aquinas, *De veritate* translated by Robert Mulligan, S.J., vol. I, q 1, a 1, 7.

Bearers of practical truth also include activities of various sorts which are called true when they live up to their ideal standards. Thus, swimmers' actions are true when they conform to correct form in swimming. In addition, one's spoken or written statements are practically (and morally) true just when they conform to one's beliefs. In all this, outer things, activities or products map or live up to their corresponding inner models as sources. By contrast in theoretical truth inner entities i.e. ideas and judgments, map their corresponding outer models as sources. Thus, our judgments are true when they correspond to things.[18] As ideas are the ground and models of things in practical truth, things or facts are the ground and models of ideas in theoretical truth.

However, if under the two-truth theory truth is in minds it follows that real things like artifacts and human activities are called true only in a secondary and extended sense, i.e. only because they copy their respective mental standards. They are also secondarily true since they are measured by those standards. As for the standards themselves such as Phidias' model of *Athena*, these are secondarily if properly speaking true. For though they measure the works that copy them, these art-models are themselves measured. But nothing the truth of which is measured by another is primarily speaking true.[19] Even though they measure and are not measured by their corresponding artifacts, art-models feed on other ideas that are drawn from experience. However novel the model of *Athena* is, it not *a priori*. It is derived from women or images of other goddesses with whom Phidias was acquainted. Similarly, true judgments such as "The *Athena* was cut by Phidias" are caused or measured by a corresponding fact, where 'cause' has the sense of a real as opposed to an ideal exemplar.

So while true judgments in theoretical truth join ideal models in practical truth in being properly speaking true, they nonetheless fall below ideal models in their degree of truth. Instead of measuring the real as do ideal art-models, judgments are measured by the real. Our judgments do not measure facts but facts measure our judg-

---

[18] St. Thomas Aquinas, *De veritate* translated by Robert Mulligan, S.J. vol. I, q 1, a 3, 13.

[19] Aquinas holds that truth is primarily and properly speaking found in God alone. See St. Thomas Aquinas, *De veritate*, trans. by R. Mulligan, S.J., vol. I, q 1, a 4, 17.

ments. So being always caused and never cause, theoretical truth ranks lower than practical truth in this hierarchy of truth. In fact, from the standpoint of being cause or measure, our judgments (though not the minds that make them) rank last among things we call true.[20] For their truth is always effect and never cause. Ideal models are exemplary causes of art works, natural things are exemplary causes of our ideas of them and even artifacts are exemplary causes of ideas of them in those who know but do not make them. But though facts are exemplary causes of true judgments, true judgments are never exemplary causes of facts, natural things or artifacts.[21]

Within practical truth, the idea of ontological truth or the conformity of natural things to God's Ideas of them adds a neo-Platonic and/or Augustinian dimension to truth. This looms large in the thought of St. Anselm who distinguished three levels of truth, i.e. the highest truth or truth that is measure only (divine truth), a middle truth or truth that is both measure and measured (the truth of things), and the lowest truth or truth that never measures but is always measured (propositional truth).[22] And despite his Aristotelianism Aquinas adopted this Anselmian division.[23]

III

From this medieval two-truth theory, a number of philosophers dissent. Moved in part by Ockham's razor, they go by the one-truth theory under which 'true' applies to judgments or propositions alone, all else being called true in an extended sense. True, these philosophers might agree that propositional truth is caused by what is

---

[20] St. Thomas Aquinas, *De veritate*, translated by R. Mulligan, S.J., vol. I, q I, a 2, 11.

[21] St. Anselm makes this point about judgments and statements. See St. Anselm, *Dialogue on Truth* in Richard McKeon, editor and translator, *Selections From Medieval Philosophers* (New York: Charles Scribner's Sons, 1929), vol. I, chapter X, 170.

[22] St. Anselm, *Dialogue on Truth*, chapter X, 170.

[23] St. Thomas Aquinas, *De veritate*, trans. by R. Mulligan, S.J., vol. I, q 1, a 2, 11.

the case. But if propositions alone are straightforwardly true, then it is nonsense to say that they are secondarily true even if they are so caused. Thus they deny Aquinas' (as well as Anselm's and other medieval realists) idea of a hierarchy of truth and of an independent ontological truth. As to the latter, they deny for example that something is called true platinum because it conforms to the Idea of platinum in God's mind or anywhere else. It is so called only because it is apt to elicit the true statement, "That is platinum".

Nevertheless, what challenges the one-truth theory is that practical truth can be a condition of theoretical (propositional) truth. And that is excluded if the former simply feeds off the latter. Suppose that Phidias cuts several false *Athenas* before completing what he calls the true one. Pointing to the latter, assume that he says to friends, "That is the true *Athena*". It is a condition of the propositional truth of his statement that the word 'true' in it means "conforms to my ideal model" which is a non-propositional sense of 'true'. If the statue were not true in that non-propositional sense but was among Phidias' failures, then Phidias' statement would in the propositional sense be false instead of true. But under the one-truth theory it is the other way around. The propositional sense of 'true' is the condition of its non-propositional senses all of which are purely derivative of it. Thus a gem is called a true diamond only because a true judgment can be made about it, i.e. "This is a diamond". For under that view 'true' is predicated of judgments alone and of other things only by reference to judgments. As, therefore, practical truth can be a condition of propositional truth, then the former is not derived from but independent of the latter. No concept that is the condition of another can be wholly derived from and hence conditioned by that other. And that means that the one-truth theory is too narrow. We should say instead with two-truth theorists that truth is the agreement of mind *and* thing, a definition that catches both truths, the truth of judgments and the truth of things.

The same follows from the side of falsehood. When Phidias says that one of his rejects which his friends see is a false and not the true *Athena*, it is evident that he calls it false because, unlike the true one, it fails to match his ideal model. True, the botch might elicit the false judgment, "That is the *Athena*". But no one believes that that is why Phidias calls it false. Not just that, but the judgment, "That is the *Athena*" is one which neither Phidias nor anyone else can make about the reject. Being directly acquainted with his own ideal model, Phidias is infallible as to whether one of his works copies it. Nor can others make that judgment either with or without knowing that what they see is one of Phidias' rejects. Not with that knowledge because then their judgment contradicts what they know is true. And not without that knowledge either since, unacquainted with both the real *Athena* and Phidias' idea of it, they are in no position to judge that what they see is the *Athena*. The judgment simply cannot arise in either case. But then the one-truth theory that truth is said only elliptically of non-judgments like works of art implies the ogre that Phidias' botch is called false because it is tied to a phantom judgment which no one can make.

All of this works against saying that when called true any non-judgment *whatsoever* includes in its sense some reference to a true judgment. But that is exactly what is implied by the one-truth theory. It follows that 'true' and 'false' do not apply strictly to judgments or propositions alone. Not all cases in which we assign 'true' and 'false' to non-judgments can be accommodated by the one-truth theory.

Yet the wider or two-truth theory under which truth is the agreement of mind *and* thing keeps the idea of some one-truth theorists that truth is mind-dependent. Things are called true only after their truth which resides in the ideal exemplars to which they conform. They are called true to their source because the latter is their truth. Recall Phidias' plea that friends view the true *Athena* and not his uncompleted rejects. He clearly calls it true because it conforms to its truth i.e. his ideal model. And if in this way the truth of something is measured by another, then it is secondarily and not primarily true.[24]

IV

A cue to specifying the common core of theoretical and practical truth (i.e. the conformity of thought and thing) comes from the truth of artifacts. Artists call their creations true or false depending on whether or not they match their ideal models as goals. Pre-existing

---

[24] St. Thomas Aquinas, *De veritate*, translated by R. Mulligan, S.J., vol. I, q 1, a 2, 11; q 1, a 4, 17.

patterns in mind are what they strive to replicate in matter. Thus the form of *Athena* as end in Phidias' psyche draws and directs his chisel like a magnet to copy that form in stone.

That suggests construing the genus "conformity of mind and thing" teleologically. Recall the idea of an end or final cause. It both precedes and causes the causality of the efficient cause and follows the latter as copy of that pre-existing end. Thus, the shape of *Athena* in Phidias' mind precedes his sculpturing as final cause of the latter and follows his sculpturing as real copy of that ideal goal. It is what draws and guides Phidias' chisel. By the same token, it is facts themselves which as real model-ends draw us to map them in our judgments about them. It is the fact itself that he cut the *Athena* in two days that draws out of Phidias the judgment or statement that he did so. Ordinary language reflects this when we call things true because they elicit true judgments or statements, as we call gold true because it elicits the true statement "That is gold". Here, the word 'elicit' has the sense of 'draw' or 'attract' and what draws or attracts is an end. Thus, as the form of *Athena* draws Phidias to recreate it in stone, so too does the fact that he cut the *Athena* in two days draw out of Phidias his judgment or statement to that effect. The difference is that while in the first a thing conforms to a goal *in mente* (practical truth) as *Athena* copies Phidias' mental model, in the second a mind conforms to a goal *in re* (theoretical truth) as Phidias' judgment matches the fact in question.[25] In the first the ideal measures the real while in the second the real measures the ideal. But in both the model, whether ideal or real, is the final cause of the copy. The agreement of mind and thing in both truths is thus spelled out in terms of result to end, of telic object to *telos*. What conforms is to what is conformed to as copy to teleological model. Thus Anselm notes that statements are true when they do what they ought to do or what it is right for them to do.[26] And the "ought to" here is teleological just as it is in practical truth when an artifact turns out as it ought to turn out, i.e. as matching its model.

---

[25] One exception is a portrait in which artists' models are real persons.
[26] St. Anselm, *Dialogue on Truth*, chapter two, 152–156.

V

It remains to see how both truths, which share this genus of conformity to a model-end, relate to knowledge. Here two questions emerge. First A), how do theoretical and practical truth relate, respectively, to theoretical and practical knowledge? And B) as within theoretical truth, how does knowledge of things relate to knowledge of truth i.e. knowledge of the agreement of judgments to things?

As to A), truth is evidently wider than its corresponding knowledge in theoretical truth. One can truly believe that P without knowing that P. Yet knowledge is equivalent to truth in the case of simple apprehension. Suppose that S has a true concept of jaguars, so that her idea of them corresponds to what they are. Then S evidently knows what jaguars are. Conversely, if S knows what jaguars are then there is conceptual truth. Her concept of the cat corresponds to the cat itself. So when it concerns the truth of concepts, truth is equivalent to its corresponding knowledge i.e. knowledge of things or knowledge-*what*. But it is different with the truth of judgment. In the latter, in which theoretical truth in us properly consists,[27] truth and knowledge are inequivalent. If S knows that Smith is seated then it is true that he is seated. But if S truly judges that he is seated then, unlike the truth of concepts, no corresponding knowledge is implied since S might only merely truly believe that he is seated.

Even so, knowledge of some sort always accompanies truth. In her judgment that Smith is seated, then, even though S might not know this, S nonetheless knows or is acquainted with Smith. If, trying to recall whether Smith was present at last week's meeting, S judges truly that he was, then even though S might only believe and not know that he was present, S nonetheless again has acquaintance with Smith. So any true judgment on the part of a person S implies that S simply apprehends or has some knowledge of the individual subject of that judgment, in this case Smith.

However, the case is both the same and different in practical truth. Practical truth is sometimes equivalent to its corresponding knowledge and sometimes not. Suppose that Phidias calls his *Athena* (practically) true because it matches his ideal model. That means

---

[27] St. Thomas Aquinas, *De veritate*, trans. by R. Mulligan, S.J., vol. I, q 1, a 3, 13; *Summa theologiae*, trans. Thomas Gilby, O.P., Ia q 16, a 2, vol. IV, 78–81.

that he is acquainted with both the artifact and model. Yet since Phidias knows his ideal model before cutting it in stone, then since there is (as yet) no artifact, then neither is there any agreement of artifact and model. But it is in the latter that practical truth consists. It follows that there is here artistic knowledge without artistic truth. Thus, whereas there can be theoretical truth without the accompanying theoretical knowledge but not *vice versa*, there cannot be practical truth without the accompanying practical knowledge even though there can be practical knowledge without the accompanying practical truth. So while theoretical truth is wider than its corresponding theoretical knowledge, practical knowledge is wider than its corresponding practical truth.

As to B) or the relation between knowing things and knowing truth or the agreement of our mind to things,[28] suppose that from observing a single triangle, a tenth-grader comes to believe (but not know) that the exterior angle formed by extending the lines of the base and side is equal to its corresponding interior angle. She might then come to a proof of that proposition and hence come to know and not just believe it. Assuming that it is better to know something than merely to believe it, we can then say that her mind improves on its prior state of belief. Mind gains by knowing as over against merely believing. But in addition, mind advances even further when, due to this newly acquired knowledge, it knows not just the geometrical fact in question but its own truth or conformity to the fact. Mind thus reflexively knows its own conformity to facts by knowing facts. Thus Aquinas identifies the end of mind not with either truth or knowledge *per se* but with the synthesis of both. This is known truth or truth *as known*.[29] This known truth is a concrete whole which includes both truth and knowledge.[30] In any case the end of mind is not truth but known truth or truth as known which consists in mind's knowing "its own conformity to the thing known." (*Intellectus autem*

---

[28] Aquinas states that mind knows its own truth in reflecting on its own act, not just as knowing its own act but also as knowing the proportion of its act to the thing. See St. Thomas Aquinas, *De veritate,* translated by R. Mulligan, S.J., vol. I, q I a 9, 41.

[29] St. Thomas Aquinas, *Summa theologiae,* trans. by Thomas Gilby, O.P., Ia, q 16, a 2, vol. IV, 78–81.

[30] This is not to suggest and no one would say that Aquinas was an Hegelian before Hegel.

conformitatem sui ad rem intelligibilem cognoscere potest; ...).[31] And mind knows its own conformity to the thing known according to him only in its second operation of judgment and not in its first operation of simple apprehension.[32]

Known truth implies and is implied by truth and knowledge-that taken together. When the tenth-grader truly believes but does not know the geometrical fact in question then she has no acquaintance with the agreement of her judgment of the fact to the fact that makes her judgment true. She lacks *known* truth. Otherwise she would know and not merely believe that fact. But when she advances from truly believing to knowing that fact, only then does she grasp the agreement of her judgment to the fact that grounds its truth.

Thus, while the truth of any judgment or proposition P implies neither one's knowledge that-P nor one's acquaintance with the truth of P, one's knowledge that-P for its part both implies and is implied by P's truth plus one's acquaintance with that truth.

VI

To summarize: the one-truth theory that truth as the conformity of mind to thing is too narrow. One should say instead that truth is the conformity of mind and thing[33], a formula which admits both likeness of mind to thing in theoretical truth and likeness of thing to mind in practical truth. This two-truth theory is justified by the example of Phidias which shows that the truth of things is sometimes a condition of the truth of judgment. But that excludes making the truth of things simply derivative of the truth of judgment which defines the one-truth theory. Moreover, whether it is the conformity of artifact to model, action to standard, statement to belief, etc., the

---

[31] St. Thomas Aquinas, *Summa theologiae*, translated by Thomas Gilby, O.P., Ia, q 16, a 2, vol. IV, 78–81.

[32] St. Thomas Aquinas, *Summa theologiae*, Ia, q 16, a 2, vol. IV, 78–81. See also, St. Thomas Aquinas, *Commentary on the Metaphysics of Aristotle*, translated by J.P. Rowan (Chicago: 1961, Henry Regnery Co.), vol. II, no. 1236, 482. (emphasis and parentheses mine).

[33] St. Thomas Aquinas, *De veritate*, translated by R. Mulligan, S.J., vol. I, q 1, a 1, 6; q 1, a 3, 13; *Summa theologiae*, translated by Thomas Gilby, O.P., Ia, q 16, a 1, 74–78.

conformity of thing to ideal model-end in practical truth cues us that the wider account of truth as the conformity of mind and thing is to be understood teleologically. In both theoretical and practical truth the terms of the conformity-relation are some *telos* and what is made after it. The difference is that this telic relation runs in opposite directions. In practical truth it is either the likeness of a real construct of ours (such as an artifact) to its mental model as end or the likeness of a real creature of God's (such as a natural thing) to its mental model as end, the latter being a divine Idea. But in theoretical truth it is always the likeness of a mental construct of ours (such as a judgment) to its real model as end, such as the fact which grounds and elicits the judgment.

Moreover, in practical truth there can be knowledge without truth. For artists know their models before they copy them, whether those models are real or ideal. Therefore, whereas practical truth implies knowledge of models, knowledge of models does not imply practical truth. But in theoretical truth it works the other way around. Since it might express mere true belief, judgmental truth does not imply knowledge-*that*. But knowledge-*that* does imply judgmental truth.

Finally, as within theoretical truth, while no proposition's truth implies either one's knowledge of that proposition or one's acquaintance with that proposition's truth, still, one's knowledge of a proposition both implies and is implied by that proposition's truth coupled with one's acquaintance with that truth. If there is known truth only when there is knowledge-*that* and if knowledge-*that* implies known truth and hence truth, then it follows that known truth or truth as known is equivalent to knowledge-*that*.

Chapter Three
Are We Drawn to the Truth?

The last chapter located the common core of practical and theoretical truth in the idea of conformity to a model-end. Practical truth is the conformity of the real to an ideal model or exemplar as end while theoretical truth is the conformity of the ideal or mental to a real model or exemplar as end. In the former truth is measure of the real while in the latter the real or facts are the measure of truth. Yet ultimately speaking, at least according to a philosopher like Aquinas, the real or facts themselves – even though they measure our minds – are for their part measured by Ideas or truth in God's mind.[34] Thus do facts in the world copy divine Ideas as their model-ends just as i) ideas or truths in us copy facts in the world as their model-ends and ii) artifacts copy their model-ends in artists' minds. Be that as it may, the present chapter begins with reasoning. It argues that it is the effect of true conclusions as they subsist as ends in God's Mind. It is truth in God that draws out of us as end the reasoning by which we reach those same truths as conclusions of that reasoning.

To begin, reasoning is the efficient cause of conclusions but conclusions are the final causes of reasoning. The relation is like that between exercise and health to which Aristotle drew our attention. Exercise is the efficient cause of health but health is the reason or final cause of exercise. Yet conclusions are not subjective ends, either explicit or implicit, in reasoners' minds. The former makes all reasoning futile. The latter fails to explain why we argue one way toward one conclusion rather than another way toward a different one. By analogy, suppose that the house toward which a builder builds is not explicitly but only implicitly in his mind as end. Then since many house-models are implicitly in his mind, nothing explains why he builds just the way he does toward that particular house and not another. Therefore, conclusions are the objective ends of reasoning. They draw our reasoning to them as the external and not the internal ends of our reasoning.

[34] St. Thomas Aquinas, *De veritate*, Q. 1 a. 2.

That conclusions are the objective ends of reasoning also follows from the status of reasoning as an immanent as opposed to a transeunt change. Immanent changes can only be caused, as by an efficient cause, by other such changes or else they are not immanent but transeunt changes. To avoid a regress, a first immanent change f in a chain of such changes as efficient causes must be posited. But since f is itself caused and the cause of f is no further efficient cause, immanent or transeunt, then a cause of a different kind must be admitted. That suggests a final cause or end. Moreover, to skirt the dilemma of ends, this final cause must transcend and not be immanent in the changes it elicits. However, only truth is plausibly said to be the end of reasoning. Therefore, the status of reasoning or arguments as immanent changes implies objective truths as the ends or final causes of those arguments.

I

The preceding is but the skeleton of the argument. To fill it in one might begin with C.S. Peirce. The latter once asked how in its relatively short history science could have found so many true hypotheses among the heaps of false ones. He ruled out chance since the possible theories in his view "exceed a trillion", and so the chances of hitting upon the true one in any given case are exceedingly slim. He concluded that the most reasonable explanation is that we have a natural bent for picking out the true theory from the nearly innumerable false ones, i.e. that working scientists have a kind of "eye for the truth." If we think "that every little chicken, that is hatched, has to rummage through all possible theories until it lights upon the good idea of picking up something and eating it"[35] says he, then even more should we deny that scientists need to sift through piles of false hypotheses before striking upon the true one.[36] If the universe conforms to general laws and our minds have developed under their influence, then, says Peirce, it is unsurprising that we "should have a

---

[35] Charles Hartshorne and Paul Weiss editors, *Collected Papers of Charles Sanders Peirce* (Cambridge: Harvard University Press, 1960) 5.591, 414–415.
[36] Hartshorne and Weiss, *Collected Papers*, 5.591, 414–415.

natural light, or *light of nature,* or *instinctive insight,* or genius, tending to make us guess those laws aright, or nearly aright".[37]

Peirce does not go so far as to say that the laws of nature are explicitly innate or that they are innate in the sense that apart from sensation, our minds can on their own turn potential knowledge of them into actual knowledge. Nor does he hold that these same laws which he says we have an instinctive capacity to discover, are transcendent ends to which we are drawn – ends which are either primordially in a transcendent Mind or in a Platonic heaven. They are in fact in his view non-absolute and evolving.[38] Besides, with Hegelians he shuns all hard and fast dualisms in metaphysics, including that between transcendent ends and worldly events or changes which those ends supposedly attract and direct.[39] Instead, Peirce explains scientists' instinctive tendency to know the laws of nature by combining scholastic realism with holism.[40] While it goes too far to count him as an Hegelian, he was sympathetic to idealistic holism, characterizing it as the "one intelligible theory of the universe"[41] Further, he held that the laws of nature (which exemplify what he called the category of thirdness) characterize nature itself as opposed to either transcending nature like Platonic forms or being foisted on nature by us. Thus Peirce is a scholastic realist on the status of universal laws as opposed to either a Platonist on the one hand or either a nominalist or conceptualist on the other.[42] These laws permeate nature making it rational throughout.

But if scientists especially look for law-like patterns in the rational whole which is Nature, and if together with those patterns they share in that whole as organic parts, then scientists are particularly drawn to or prone to grasp nature's laws. Thus does Peirce's realistic holism as regards laws and our relation to them involve a veiled teleology.[43] Scientists are drawn to those laws just because

---

[37] Hartshorne and Weiss, *Collected Papers,* 5.604, 421.
[38] Hartshorne and Weiss, *Collected Papers,* 6.101, 84. See also, 6.13, 15.
[39] Hartshorne and Weiss, *Collected Papers,* 6.26, 20.
[40] Peirce states that pragmaticism, with some differences, is "closely allied to the Hegelian absolute idealism." (*Collected Papers,* 5.436, 291).
[41] Hartshorne and Weiss, *Collected Papers,* 6.25, 20.
[42] Hartshorne and Weiss, *Collected Papers,* 5.93–5.101.
[43] Peirce's attitude toward teleology is mixed. Though he states that "...science can only allow itself to be swayed by efficient causes...", (*Collected*

they are in a sense one with them. The laws are instinctively in them just because rational Nature lives in both, uniting them as the life of a vine unites its branches. The laws attract their discoverers just because rational Nature which those laws characterize are in those discoverers as any organic whole is in its parts. Peirce's realistic holism comes out in his statement to the effect that since general laws and ideas hold throughout the universe and an inquirer's mind "is itself a product of this universe", then these same laws are "by logical necessity incorporated in his own being"[44]

Be that as it may, it seems that a wider and externally teleological answer to Peirce's query might be proffered. First and as to breadth, though Peirce might be right that researches in science are drawn to the truth, does this obtain just in the matter of framing scientific hypotheses in which Peirce evidently had special interest? Or does this attraction to truth hold across the board in reasoning, i.e. not just among inquiring scientists but among all of us in our everyday lives? Moreover, might not that attraction extend beyond laws or what Peirce called thirds to include more specific truths of fact as well? Second and as to teleology, might it also be true that we are drawn to the truth not because Nature and her laws are in us as an organic whole is in its parts but because some external end or ends attract our reason to the truth? Not just that, but since we reason for the sake of true conclusions, might not these very conclusions be the ends to which our reason is drawn? To answer these questions affirmatively, one might begin not with reason in science but with ordinary practical reason in ethics.

II

Suppose that going by the rule that one ought to act according to right reason in almsgiving, Jane correctly judges that giving five-hundred dollars to famine relief meets right reason in her case given the need and her own resources. From this suppose that she con-

Papers, 6.434, 304) he also holds that "...physical evolution works toward ends in the same way that mental action works toward ends, and thus in one aspect of the matter it would be perfectly true to say that final causality is alone primary." (Collected Papers, 6.101, 84.)

[44] Collected Papers, 5.603, 421.

cludes that it is her duty is to donate that sum. Call Jane's practical reason R and its true conclusion C. Insofar as C prescribes an action which in Jane's case gets between stinginess and extravagance, C exemplifies right reason in almsgiving. So C is a moral truth about Jane. And insofar as Jane acts on C, her action conforms to right reason and so is morally right. Here, Jane's acting on a practical syllogism exemplifies what might be called the triad of ends in ethics. First comes practical reason, in this case R. As an instance of reasoning, R actuates Jane's difference among animals which is the capacity for reason. But if actuating a difference perfects a subject insofar as it has that differentiating capacity, then R perfects Jane as having the natural bent to reason.[45] By analogy, to the extent that sculpturing actuates a sculptor's difference among artisans which is having the art of or the capacity for sculpture, then sculpturing perfects the sculptor as having that difference. R is thus the good of Jane *qua* having the bent to reason just as sculpturing is the good of sculptors *qua* having the bent to sculpture. And if good has the nature of an end, then R is the end of Jane as having the difference of or natural capacity for reason. Second comes C. For though itself end with respect to our difference and bent toward it, reasoning itself has an end which is a known conclusion, in this case C. We reason from what is more directly known as premises to conclusions that are indirectly known through those premises. And we do so for the sake of knowing those conclusions. Finally there is the final (and properly speaking) ethical end in this triad of ends. That is Jane's choice to act upon C. This is the action by which Jane carries out C. Thus, since practical reason is for practical truth and the latter is for right choices, then Jane's choosing to do what C prescribes is the final end in this teleological triad.

---

[45] The idea of the actual perfecting the potential and hence being the good of the latter is a common theme in Aristotelian–Thomistic thought. So is the idea that an end has the nature of good. As to the latter, an end is act with respect to some potentiality toward it. Recall Aristotle's example of man which as end or final cause of the generation of a man, actualizes the potentiality in the generator to generate. (Aristotle, *Physics*, in J. L. Ackrill, editor, *A New Aristotle Reader* (Princeton: Princeton University Press, 1987), Book 2, chapter 7 198a, 25–28, 105–106). But since act realizes and so perfects potentiality, act is the good of potentiality. So an end has the nature of good with respect to that of which it is the end.

That the first link in this triad, R, is for the sake of knowing C means that the latter is the end or final cause of R. Taking this as a datum, it further follows that besides being in Jane as known conclusion of and as temporally following R, C logically precedes R. If knowing C is the end of R and any end is prior to that of which it is the end, then knowing C is logically prior to R. Yet as end of R, knowledge of C is not prior to R in Jane's mind. Otherwise Jane already knows what she uses R to know, making R futile.

To block this, it might be denied that the end of Jane's syllogism is C. Instead, it is some unspecified conclusion s that is as yet unknown and that this end is evidently in Jane prior to her reasoning. Thus, the end in all our reasoning is not a specific conclusion but some true conclusion or other, s. This end exists in our minds as the goal of our reasoning and in that capacity it precedes that reasoning as any end precedes the means or process toward it. What Jane knows prior to R is not R's conclusion C but her own goal of new knowledge s through reason. Like all of us, Jane looks to acquire new knowledge from existing knowledge.

Though *prima facie* plausible, this objection confuses the end of reasoning generally, i.e. new conclusions, with the end of R. True, knowledge of some unspecified conclusion s is the end of reasoning generally, and like any end this both precedes and follows the process toward it. Abstractly considered, reasoning has knowledge of a conclusion as its initial purpose and as its end-result. However, it is not reason in the abstract which is here concerned but Jane's specific syllogism R. So to say that R has s for its conclusion commits the fallacy of false abstraction. The conclusion of R is evidently C and not some unspecified conclusion, s. But as ends precede the means or processes toward them, it follows that C precedes as well as follows R.

Put differently, the objection makes a half-truth into the whole truth. True, apart from actually reasoning, Jane's goal as potential reasoner is to come to know some unspecified conclusion. Yet no sooner does Jane begin to reason *via* R than R assumes the specific goal C. Compare this to a carpenter Jake who, being hired by Jack to build a house, shows Jack many models of homes from which to choose. At this stage as potentially building, Jake's goal is to build an as yet unspecified house. But once Jake begins to build, his building B has a certain house H as its goal which is first in Jake's mind and last *in re*. As it is with B so is it with R. As it is nonsense to say that at this consequent stage Jake's goal is an unspecified house, so too is it nonsense to say that consequent to Jane's beginning to reason via R the end of R is some unspecified conclusion s.

Continuing the analogy with B makes this clear. If Jake's end in B is some house or other, then nothing explains the fact that Jake builds this way and not that, i.e. B-ly and not say, B'-ly. But Jake evidently builds at every stage B-ly and not otherwise due to H. The end determines the shape, form and course of the means.[46] Similarly, if Jane's end in R is some conclusion or other then nothing explains the fact that Jane reasons this way and not that, i.e. R-ly and not say, R'-ly. No unspecified conclusion explains the specific form or course of R, i.e. that Jane's reasoning takes just this form and not another and has just these premises and not others. Moreover, as the physical process B is incomplete and so imperfect until it reaches its specific end H, so too is the mental process R incomplete and so imperfect until it reaches its end which as was said is not "some knowledge or other" but knowledge that-C. Finally, just as H as end of B precedes B or else B is not for the sake of H, so too does C as end of R precede R or else R is not for the sake of C.

Yet like all analogies this one limps. For the difference between B and R is that while H precedes B in Jake's mind, C does not precede R in Jane's mind. Otherwise R is futile since Jane already knows before R what she uses R to learn. Still, as end of R, C does precede R or else nothing explains the fact that Jane reasons R-ly and not otherwise. That just goes to the definition of an end or final cause as logically first, i.e. as grounding the form, course and direction of the efficient cause.[47]

A third possibility falls between Jane's end in R being explicitly C and its being some unspecified true conclusion s. It is that Jane's

---

[46] Aquinas holds that in practical matters like morals the end is in the position of a principle in speculative matters. See St. Thomas Aquinas, *Summa theologiae*, Thomas Gilby, editor, vol. 17, I b, Q. 8, a. 2, 54–57; see also *Summa theologiae*, vol. 17, I b, Q. 9, a. 3, 68–71.

[47] Aquinas states that the final cause is the cause of the causality of the efficient cause. See St. Thomas Aquinas, *The Principles of Nature* in Forrest Baird and Walter Kaufmann, editors, *Medieval and Renaissance Philosophy* (Upper Saddle River, N.J: Pearson Prentice Hall, 2008), chapter 4, (24), 405. See also, St. Thomas Aquinas, *Summa theologiae*, Thomas Gilby, editor, vol. 2, I a, Q. 5, a. 4, 71–73.

end in *R* is *C as implicit* in Jane's mind. In other words, Jane moves in *R* from implicitly knowing *C* at the start of *R* to explicitly knowing *C* at the close of *R*. Thus, since at the outset of *R* Jane's knowledge of *C* is not explicit but only implicit, *R* escapes futility. Jane does not already explicitly know what she uses *R* to discover and so her syllogism *R* escapes futility. At the same time, since Jane's unconscious end in *R* is not some unspecified conclusion *s* but specifically *C*, then the objection of confusing the end of *R* with that of reasoning generally goes by the board. Under this assay, then, all of our conclusions are initially so many innate ideas in a kind of Leibnizian sense which lay dormant in and unattended to by us until the occasion arises for us to think of them in an explicit way. And in Jane's case, that occasion is *R*. Recall Leibniz' agreement with Plato that the soul knows truths virtually "and requires only *attention* to recognize truths, and that, consequently, it has, at the very least, the ideas upon which these truths depend."[48]

Compared with the first two options, this third account might appear attractive. Yet as implicitly known by Jane, *C* is not the end of *R*. True, prior to *R* *C* might be implicitly in Jane. But that implicit conclusion is not the end of *R*. It is not for the sake of knowing conclusions implicitly that we reason but for the sake of knowing them explicitly. Otherwise nothing is gained since we move from the implicitly known to the implicitly known. Thus would reasoning again be futile. But this time it is futile not because conclusions are already explicitly known by reasoners but because it moves from an implicitly known conclusion to the same implicitly known conclusion. But if anything we move in reasoning from knowing conclusions implicitly to the end of knowing them explicitly. So, not being in the first place the end of *R*, Jane's prior implicit knowledge of *R*'s conclusion is no more what draws or elicits that conclusion out of Jane than does her prior explicit knowledge of that conclusion. Besides, that the end of *R* is *C* as implicit in Jane fails to explain why Jane argues *R*-ly and not otherwise. For suppose that *C* exists as a mere implicit end in Jane's mind. Then, since many other conclusions also exist in her as implicit ends of her reasoning, then nothing explains why Jane reasons just

---

[48] Gottfried Leibniz, *Discourse on Metaphysics* in Roger Ariew and Daniel Garber, translators, *Philosophical Essays* (Indianapolis & Cambridge: Hackett Publishing Co., 1989), # 26, 58. It is to be noted, however, that Leibniz dissents from Plato's view of the preexistence of the soul.

one way (R–ly) for C and not another way (R'–ly) for a different conclusion (say D). By analogy, suppose that the model of *Athena* toward which Phidias works exists as a mere implicit end in Phidias' mind. Then since many other models also exist as implicit ends in him (say models of his future works such as *Zeus*), then no account is given of why Phidias works his chisel just one way for *Athena* and not another way for *Zeus*.[49] And yet the rub is that it is not *her* explicit knowledge of C that is the final cause of her reasoning R or else R is futile.

What then is the solution? Evidently it is one which both affirms that C is the end of R and yet denies that that end is identified with C either as explicitly in Jane or as mere implicit end in her. What might seem to satisfy both *desiderata* is C's being identified with a fact that is independent of minds. However, the end of intellectual activity is knowledge and so Jane's end in R is not a fact but knowledge of a fact or some truth. We reason for the sake of true conclusions. But the latter are not facts but facts as assimilated to intellect. Therefore, if facts themselves are the ends of reasoning then either we do not reason for the sake of true conclusions or else reasoning has two ends. But the former is self-evident and the latter is unacceptable.

To satisfy both *desiderata*, therefore, it is hypothesized that C subsists in an external mind M as the end or final cause of R.[50] Under this assay, though moral truths like C exist in us when we reach them by practical reason, they none the less subsist by logical priority as ends in M. The difference is that they are model-ends in M and cop-

---

[49] The difference in the two cases is that while the explicitly known end, i.e. the ideal model of *Athena*, is in Phidias' mind preceding his carving, the explicitly known conclusion does not exist in Jane's mind preceding her reasoning. Otherwise her reasoning R is futile. Still by our argument, it none the less does precede R and is the end of the latter in an external Mind M.

[50] Many philosophers have held that truth is in minds. Truth is where falsehood is and the latter is in minds. Otherwise one not only risks the oddity of objective falsehoods but also (since falsehood then has objective status) threatens to blur the distinction between truth and falsehood. See St. Thomas Aquinas *De Veritate*, in Richard McKeon, editor, *Selections from Medieval Philosophers* (New York: Charles Scribners Sons, 1958) Q.1, a. 2,170–174. See also, St. Thomas Aquinas, *Summa theologiae*, Thomas Gilby, editor (London: Blackfriars, in conjunction with Eyre & Spottiswoode, 1964), vol. 4, I a, Q. 16, a. 1, 74–78; I a, Q, 17, a. 1, 100–101. Also see Russell, B. *The Problems of Philosophy* (London: Home University Library, Oxford University Press, 1912) chapter 12.

ies in us.⁵¹ This follows the scholastic dictum that ends are first in mind as exemplars and last in things (or other minds) as *exemplata*. In addition, they are known non-discursively by M. Otherwise like us M is a finite mind that moves from potentiality to actuality in knowledge. Not just that but if they are in M discursively then by our account M is drawn to them as ends by another Mind, and if the latter knows those same truths only discursively then it too is drawn to them as ends by still another Mind, and so on *ad infinitum*. So it is that moral truths like *C* are by priority in M as ends to which we like Jane are inclined by reason. Thus do these same truths as well as our coming to know them depend on M.

III

Our hypothesis gains strength from *R*'s status as an immanent activity. Aquinas, for one, contrasts what have come to be known as immanent and transeunt activities as follows:

> There are, however, two sorts of operation, as Aristotle teaches in *Metaphysics* IX: one that remains in the agent and is a perfection of it, as the act of sensing, understanding, and willing; another that passes over into an external thing, and is a perfection of the thing made as a result of that operation, the acts of heating, cutting and building, for example.⁵²

In this distinction Aquinas follows Aristotle.⁵³ The second kind of activity to which Aquinas refers (transeunt activities) begins in

---

⁵¹ This recalls but is not identical with Leibniz' idea that the sequence of ideas in us follows a divine plan. This is part of his celebrated theory of the pre-established harmony of the monads.

⁵² Aquinas, *Summa contra gentiles*, trans. J.F. Anderson (Notre Dame, IN: Univ. of Notre Dame Press, 1975) Book 2: Creation, Chapter 1, no. 2. See also, Aquinas, *Summa theologiae*, Thomas Gilby, editor, vol. 4, Foreword to I a, Q.14-18, 3.

⁵³ Aquinas is here referring to Aristotle's *Metaphysics* IX, chapter 8 (1050a) 25. Consistent with his idea of the unfolding of the monads according to an internal principle or entelechy, Leibniz also stresses the idea of immanent as opposed to transeunt activities. See G. W. Leibniz, *On Nature Itself* in Ariew and

one thing and pass over to and produces a change in another. It always issues in an effect that is outside of the efficient cause. Thus Jake's building B passes over to the house H. That means that B is not only Jake's end as having the capacity to build but has for its part the further and external end H just when Jake is considered as building. Thus two possibilities are actuated, i.e. that of Jake to build and that of building materials to become H. Here something else is being produced besides the activity.[54] A non-voluntary example is a lawn chair that is propelled against the side of a house by a tornado. Here, the possibility of the chair's being propelled is actuated and this passes over to the actuation of the house's possibility to be impacted by the chair. So once again two possibilities are realized, one in the agent and the other in the patient.

Not so according to Aquinas with the first kind of activity to which he refers (immanent activities). These both begin and end in the same thing.[55] They do not go over to and effect a change in another thing. They remain in their agents perfecting them as any end perfects that of which it is the end. In the view of Aquinas, all immanent activities are found in living things. Thus,

> ...Following a diversity of natures, one finds a diverse manner of emanation in things, and the higher a nature is, the more intimate to the nature is that which flows from it.
>
> For, in all things, inanimate bodies have the lowest place. There can be no emanations in these except by the action of some one of them on another one. For this is the way in which fire is generated by fire, when an extraneous body is changed by the fire and is brought to the quality and species of fire.[56]

Garber, translators and editors, *Philosophical Essays* (Indianapolis & Cambridge: Hackett Publishing Co., 1989), 161.

[54] For a clear contrast of transeunt and immanent activities on this point, see St. Thomas Aquinas, *Commentary on the Metaphysics of Aristotle*, trans. J.P. Rowan (Chicago: Henry Regnery Co., 1961), vol. 2, no. 1862–864, 688–89.

[55] Not all immanent operations begin and end in the same *part* of the same thing. Thus, nutrition and growth begin in one part of an organism and end in another part. However, even here the operations begin and end in the same organism.

[56] St. Thomas Aquinas, *Summa contra gentiles*, trans. Charles J. O'Neil (Garden City, N.Y: Doubleday & Co., 1957), Book 4, chapter 11, no. 1–2, 79–80.

By contrast, life or its principle the soul, is the source of immanent activities. So all of them issue from within an organism and are not simply the result of some action on the organism by another thing. In different degrees organisms are self-moved in these activities. They thus have a spontaneity which non-living things lack. By this vital power they all grow and assimilate food. Some produce eggs and seeds and move from place to place. The highest, human beings, understand, reason, will and choose. Thus,

> Life is essentially that by which a thing is able to move itself, taking the word "movement" in a wide sense, so that even the operation of the intellect can be called "movement". For, those things that can be moved only by an exterior principle are said to be without life.[57]

Unlike transeunt activities, immanent activities produce no further end besides themselves, as for instance, building produces a house.[58] They do not issue in any effect or end that is outside of their agents. Moreover, if life is the principle of self-movement and if in the view of Aquinas the soul of a living thing is its principle of its life, then it follows that the soul of a living thing is that by which it is able to move itself.

From this come the following Thomistic definitions of transeunt and immanent activities:

x is a transeunt activity in a subject, S =df (i) x actualizes a possibility in S and (ii) x passes over to and actualizes a possibility in another thing, T.

y is an immanent activity in a subject, S =df (i) y actualizes a possibility in S and (ii) y neither passes over to nor actualizes a possibility in another thing, T but ends in S and (iii) S through its soul is the efficient cause of y.

What with this distinction in place, let us return to R. Under the above definition of immanence R is an immanent activity. Reasoning begins in us and not in some external thing. Otherwise it is

---

[57] St. Thomas Aquinas, *Commentary on Aristotle's De Anima* , trans. Kenelm Foster, O.P. and Silvester Humphries, O.P. (New Haven: Yale University Press, 1965), no. 219, 168.

[58] St. Thomas Aquinas, *Commentary on the Metaphysics of Aristotle*, vol.2 no. 1862-64, 688-689.

the latter that reasons and not us. And so far from passing over to and actuating a possibility in other things as do transeunt changes like building, reason ends in us in the form of conclusions. Moreover, by reason we move ourselves under a principle to a conclusion. This parallels willing in which we move ourselves under an end to choose a means. Ends and means are in appetitibles what principles and conclusions respectively are in intelligibles.[59]

That aside, the point is that immanent activities like R are traced to M as their final cause. Though Jane is the agent cause of R, Jane as such is not the total cause of her going from potentially reasoning via R to her actually doing so. Otherwise, assuming Jane's self-identity through time and that any total cause is sufficient for its effect, Jane always reasons via R. That flouts her experience and ours that she goes from not using R to draw C to doing so. So something else is needed to cover the change. By analogy, it is not the builder Jake but the builder Jake as building that is the actual efficient cause of H's coming-to-be.[60] The question then is, what guides the causality of this actual efficient cause? What, for example, makes Phidias carve just the way he does as he moves toward his goal, i.e. the *Athena*? What guides or orders the cuts of his chisel? And in the case at hand, what makes Jane reason R-ly and not otherwise?

The evident answer to the first question is the model of *Athena* in Phidias' mind which orders the cuts of his chisel. It does so as end or final cause of the change. So it is with the second question. To repeat, what makes Jane reason R-ly and not otherwise is none other than C itself in M as final cause of R.

To see why, suppose that to cover Jane's going from potentially using R to get to C to her actually doing so without admitting final causes one has recourse to an immanent activity in Jane prior to R as efficient cause of the latter and so on back to a first immanent operation (call it f) in Jane. For its part, is f caused by a previous immanent activity in Jane or is Jane the passive recipient of f the efficient cause of which is some external thing or event T?

Neither one can be admitted. Either i) f is the effect of another immanent activity in Jane, say, f', or ii), the efficient cause of f is not

---

[59] St. Thomas Aquinas, *Summa theologiae*, Thomas Gilby editor, vol. 17, I b, Q. 9, a. 3, 68–71.

[60] Aristotle, *Physics*, in J.L. Ackrill, editor, *A New Aristotle Reader*, (195b), 4–6, 99; 195b, 16–21, 100.

Jane or Jane's soul but some external thing T. However, neither *i*) nor *ii*) is true. If *i*) is true, then *f*, the supposed first immanent activity in Jane, is not the first immanent activity in Jane. But if *ii*) is true, then *f* is not in the first place an immanent activity. For then instead of being the source of *f*, Jane is but the passive recipient of *f*. And being imposed on Jane by T, *f* is no immanent activity.[61]

So the question persists: what explains Jane's going from potentially using R to get to C to her actually doing so? The answer is none other than C itself as end or final cause of the change. As such C both precedes and follows R in different respects. C logically precedes R as the end or reason of C while R temporally precedes C as any reasoning precedes its conclusion as the latter's efficient cause. Recall the reciprocity of final and efficient causes under which the former is the cause of the causality of the latter while the latter is the cause of the former's realization *in re*.[62] As that for the sake of which an efficient cause acts to produce an effect, a final cause logically precedes both the efficient cause and the effect. Moreover, this effect copies the final cause. Thus, *Phidias'* mental model of *Athena* not only precedes both his sculpturing and the finished product but it is also the latter's model or exemplar.

Yet as known end, C is not internal but external to Jane.[63] Otherwise either R is futile or nothing explains Jane's arguing R-ly and not otherwise. Hence our hypothesis that C subsists in a transcend-

---

[61] The pattern of this argument recalls Jonathan Edwards' disproof of Arminian free choice. Edwards argued that the first free choice of the will is caused either by a preceding free choice in the will or by something outside the will. If the former, then the supposed first free choice of the will is not the first free choice of the will. But if the latter, then the supposed first free choice of the will is caused by something outside the will and hence is not free. See Jonathan Edwards, *Freedom of the Will*, in Clarence Faust and Thomas Johnson, eds. *Jonathan Edwards* (New York: Hill and Wang, 1962), Part 2, section 1, 284-286.

[62] St. Thomas Aquinas, *The Principles of Nature*, in Baird and Kaufmann, editors, *Medieval and Renaissance Philosophy*, chapter 4, (24), 404-405. See also, St. Thomas Aquinas, *Summa theologiae*, Thomas Gilby editor, vol. 2, I a, Q. 5, a. 4, 71-73.

[63] C is potentially in Jane before she reasons in terms of R and in that sense internal to her. However, C is not at this stage actually in Jane, or else R is futile.

ent Mind M in which it functions as end or final cause of R.[64] By analogy, models precede their artifacts in artisans' minds as the explicit or attended to ends of those artifacts.

Outlining this we get,

1. Jane's practical reason R is an immanent and not a transeunt change. Otherwise R does not begin and end in Jane.
2. The question then becomes, "What explains Jane's moving from potentially reasoning via R to her actually doing so"?
3. The answer is not simply Jane or else, assuming her self-identity through time, Jane always undergoes the change in question.
4. Alternatively, suppose that the cause is a prior immanent activity in Jane, say, R-1, and the cause of that a still prior such activity in Jane say, R -2, and so on back to the first immanent activity in Jane, say, f.
5. Then in that case, what explains f in Jane?
6. It is not a prior immanent activity in Jane or else f, the supposed first immanent activity in Jane, is not the first immanent activity in Jane.
7. And not some external thing T or else, T and not Jane being the source of f, f is not in the first instance an immanent activity.
8. So the question recurs: what explains Jane's going from potentially reasoning via R to her actually doing so?
9. The answer is R's conclusion C which elicits the change in question as its end or final cause, thus explaining the course of R as artisans' ideal models explain the course of their movements toward artifacts.
10. As final cause of the change, C logically precedes R. Yet, as known end, C is not explicitly in Jane or else R is futile.
11. Nor is the end C only latently in Jane as a kind of Leibnizian implicit idea. Otherwise, since Jane implicitly knows many other conclusions, nothing explains why Jane reasons R-ly and not otherwise toward some other conclusion, D. By analogy, if

---

[64] This is not to say that C functions as a conclusion in M. It does so only in Jane (or other persons) whose knowledge of most truths is discursive and not intuitive. Moreover, in Jane as in other persons conclusions, practical or theoretical, are prior to the reasoning toward them potentially though posterior to them actually.

the end, *Athena*, is only implicitly in Phidias, then nothing explains the course of Phidias' chisel toward *Athena* and not say, *Zeus*.
12. Therefore, it is hypothesized that C as known is external to Jane in M where it draws R out of Jane as end or final cause of R. By analogy, models pre-exist explicitly in artisans' minds as final causes of their artifacts and their movements toward them.

IV

Nevertheless to all of this it might be objected that our proposal excludes falsehood. If we are drawn to right reasoning by truth in M then how do we go astray and miss out on the truth? For we sometimes reason badly and end up with false beliefs. Does truth in M also draw us to reason badly? And if it does not, then does not our argument from immanence imply an alternative end or final cause of bad reasoning just as it commits us to M, the final cause of good reasoning? For whether good or bad, reasoning is an immanent activity and we argued that such activity is covered only by final causes.

The answer is that being drawn to the truth hardly implies reaching it. Being attracted to x and failing to reach x are not incompatible. Ends might go unrealized. This is often due to bad moves on our part. A team's being drawn to the end-zone is not incompatible with its failing to reach it through bad plays on the field. Yet the team is all along drawn to the goal. Plays that conduce to the end we call good and those that frustrate that end we call bad. Ordinary language thus reflects the idea that good has the nature of an end. If so, moves that lead away from the end are bad or evil, the latter being nothing but the privation of good. Similarly, our being drawn to true conclusions is compatible with our not reaching them through bad logic. In fact, the end is in each case a necessary condition of the attempted means. As athletic misplays occur only if teams are in the first place drawn to goals, so too does bad reasoning occur only if reasoners are in the first instance drawn to the goal of truth. We reason either rightly or wrongly only because we already seek true conclusions.

It might be countered that this feeds on a false analogy. For our argument concerns moving from not knowing truths to knowing them *via* arguments which are elicited from us by that those same truths in M as final cause of those arguments. Thus, though it is (as yet) unknown by her, Jane's true conclusion as it subsists external to her in M is the end or final cause of her practical syllogism R. But, so the counter would run, ends in sports and other activities are not truths. Nor are they initially unknown by us only to become known by reasoning. On the contrary they are ends which we explicitly know from the start i.e. before we exercise the means to reach them. Football players already explicitly know that their goal is the end-zone before taking means to reach it. By contrast, reasoners do not explicitly know conclusions beforehand or else all reasoning is futile. They only know that their end is some true conclusion or other.

Nevertheless this difference makes no difference. Our being drawn to some activity by a pre-conceived end scarcely implies our reaching it even when beforehand we have only general knowledge of that end. If our being drawn in argument to some truth that is as yet unknown to us implies our reaching it then no one ever reasons to false conclusions.

Therefore, as to the question whether truth in M draws us even to bad reasoning the answer is that in a sense it does. This paradox is assuaged once we distinguish bad reasoning *as reasoning* and bad reasoning *as bad or disordered*. As bad or disordered, reasoning signifies a privation in the intellect of discursive order and so is a form of intellectual evil. As bad plays on the field are called bad because they lack orientation to the end of players' moves, so too bad logical moves are called bad because they lack orientation to the end of reasoning which is true conclusions. Even so, that bad reasoning *qua* reasoning (and not *qua* bad) is drawn out of us by M as final cause follows from the immanence of reasoning. To recall the link, suppose that final causes are excluded. Suppose too that the efficient cause of a person S's bad reasoning goes back to a first immanent change f in S. Then either f is caused by a prior such change or f is caused by some event e that is external to S. If the former, then the supposed first immanent change f is not the first immanent change. But if the latter, then being the effect of e, f is not in the first instance an immanent change. Therefore it must be conceded that just to the extent that it is an immanent event, S's bad reasoning – no less than Jane's good reasoning – is elicited by M as end or final cause. It is just that due to the lack of discursive skill in S or what Aquinas calls the intellectual virtue of science, S fails to reach the truth.

So it is that though reasoning in us is the efficient cause of true conclusions in us, those same conclusions as they subsist in M are final causes of reasoning in us. Though Jane's reasoning is the efficient cause of her concluding to C, nonetheless C in M is what in the first instance draws out or is the final cause of Jane's reasoning. Thus do our true conclusions as well as our coming to know them depend on M.

To this the Father of Pragmatism himself might have assented, provided that M is not construed as transcendent. For he explained our success-rate in discovering the laws of nature in terms of realistic holism. If scientific laws permeate the world and if in addition both these laws and ourselves are organic parts of one and the same Reality so that the latter figure in our make-up, then we should be bent to discovering those laws just because the latter would be internal and not foreign to us. And that would go far to explain our success-rate in our latching onto those laws.

Nevertheless Peirce's immanent finalism, like that of Aristotle's, faces a defeating dilemma. To spell it out, consider the dilemma of such internal ends as it takes hold in the celebrated example of the acorn and oak. Either as final cause the oak pre-exists the bent of the acorn toward it or not. If not, then it can hardly instigate that bent. If so, then since it already actually is, it cannot be said that the acorn is moving toward it. Nothing tends toward what it already is.

It might seem that an Aristotelian answer to this avails. It is that the oak both pre-exists the acorn's bent toward it and does not pre-exist the acorn's bent toward it but in different respects. To the extent that it does not *actually* pre-exist the acorn's bent toward it, it can meaningfully be said that the acorn tends toward it. What does not already actually exist can be tended toward. But to the extent that the oak at least *potentially* pre-exists the acorn's bent toward it and potential existence is not simple non-existence, then the (potential) oak can instigate the acorn's movement toward being an (actual) oak. Yet the evident counter-reply here is that nothing that is only potentially the case can instigate anything actual. It takes something actual to do that, whether the cause in question is final or efficient. Phidias' mere potential end to cut the *Athena* cannot induce him begin cutting it, nor can his state of merely potentially cutting the *Athena* cause it to begin to be cut.

A clue to escaping the fork comes from human purpose where the end or final cause is external and not internal. Here, the end does pre-exist the bent toward it. However it does so not *in re* but externally *in mente* and the difference makes all the difference. So it cannot be charged that since the end already exists it is nonsense to say that something moves toward it. For the end does not already exist internally or *in re*. Thus the *Athena* pre-exists in Phidias' mind as mental model and that is quite consistent with Phidias' moving toward it with his chisel. In this way does one dissolve the dilemma, i.e. by distinguishing internal and external or mental ends and opting for the latter. However, that is just what is here being proposed except that the mind in which the end pre-exists externally is not ours but M's. And if under that same view M is identified with God, then it follows that in our coming by reason to true conclusions it is none other than God Himself Who as final cause of our reason draws both it and us to the truth.

Chapter Four
The Bearer of Truth

The last two chapters showed how the common core of theoretical and practical truth lay in the idea of an end which draws or elicits both the truth of things and the truth of judgments. It was argued that true conclusions in us are the effects of those same truths in Mind as final causes. Though our reasoning is the efficient cause of these conclusions, the latter – taken not as conclusions but as subsisting *a priori* in Mind – are the final causes of our reasoning. That aside, in addition to the questions of the sense and types of truth is that of the bearer of truth, and it is to this question that the present chapter turns.

That truth-bearers are judgments in the sense of mental entities (mentalism) is falsified by cases of straightforward truth in the absence of such entities. The question remains as to whether truth-bearers are identified with objective propositions or with the assertive use of sentences. However, the proposition-theory is untenable either when true propositions are construed as similar to and as corresponding to facts or as identified with facts. The first implies the ogre that the truth-relation is one in which proposition and fact share a common proposition, while the second commits a category mistake. Therefore, those who wish to retain the correspondence view of truth are better advised to identify truth-bearers with sentence-tokens. These are sentences used to assert that something is the case.

I

To spell all this out, as to the bearer of truth, some philosophers hold that in the logical and not the ontological sense of 'true' (i.e. "true judgment" and not "true gold")[65] truth-bearers are judgments where by 'judgments' it is meant mental entities of a kind. We can call this view about the bearer of truth mentalism. Thus Aquinas, Locke and Kant (to name a few) all hold that truth-bearers in this usual logical sense of 'true' are judgments in this sense or kinds of *entia rationis*. Whatever other objection might be raised against it (the threat of psychologism included), mentalism fails to cover truth in the absence of judgments. Recall Pablo's 'lie' in Sartre's *The Wall*.[66] Pablo's captors demand to know where the ringleader Ramon Gris, is hiding. They promise to release Pablo if he tells them the truth. Pablo answers that Gris is hiding in the gravedigger's shack in the cemetery. Openly skeptical, Pablo's captors warn him that if he is lying he will be executed. Pablo himself disbelieves his own statement but cynically utters it just to laugh at his captors as they march to the cemetery. The concluding twist is that Gris *is* hiding in the gravedigger's shack and Pablo is released because he "told the truth".

The point is that at the time at which Pablo makes his statement no one believes that what he says is true. In that case, no one judges that Gris is in the gravedigger's shack either. For if you judge that something is the case then you assent to it and hence believe it (and *vice versa*). Yet it is evident that Pablo's statement is straightforwardly true. So despite the absence of any mental entity or act like a believing or a judging on the part of either Pablo or his captors, there is nonetheless something here that is true, namely, Pablo's statement. That shows that primarily speaking the bearer of truth is not a belief or a judgment in the sense of a being of reason or mental entity.

Yet proposition-theorists or those who identify truth-bearers with the objective senses of sentences (propositions) would retort that this at best defeats mentalism. It does not show that truth-bearers are sentence-tokens. For the option remains that truth-bearers are propositions or the objective senses of sentences-tokens

---

[65] Some hold that the ontological sense of 'true' is just derivative of the logical sense. In terms of the example, they say that calling something "true gold" means nothing more than that it is something about which the true judgment, "That is gold" is made. This derivability-thesis will not here be discussed.

[66] J. P. Sartre, *The Wall*, in Walter Kaufmann, ed., *Existentialism from Dostoevsky to Sartre* (New York: Meridian Books, 1957), 239–240.

and not either sentence-tokens themselves or judgments in the sense of mental acts. But if so, then no one can use the case of Pablo to show that truth-bearers are sentence-tokens.

Still, proposition-theory has troubles of its own. One is how it is compatible with the correspondence view of truth. Under proposition-theory, if A says in English "John loves Mary" and B says in French "Jean aime Marie" when both refer to the same persons, then it is the common objective sense (proposition) expressed by each sentence that is true or false. When it is true, the proposition conforms to reality, but when it is false it fails to conform to reality. In the latter case it is taken by proposition-theorists either as having psychological being only or as being an objective falsehood. By the same token, if A and B truly believe that John loves Mary, it is once again the common objective sense (proposition), i.e. *what* they believe, that is true. This holds for all proposition-theorists, whether they are platonists or not about the status of propositions, whether they do or do not countenance objective falsehoods, and whether they do or do not identify propositions with logically necessary states of affairs.[67]

Defining truth as the conformity of propositions to reality is wide enough to catch almost any theory of truth, including coherence and pragmatic theories. But many proposition-theorists specify that characterization such that it catches only correspondence theories. Thus, they deny that a simple proposition P is true because P conforms to reality either in the sense that P coheres with a body of accepted truths or in the sense that P satisfies our goals.[68] They hold

---

[67] For an account of propositions as being logically necessary states of affairs see R. M. Chisholm, *The First Person*, (Minneapolis: University of Minnesota Press, 1981), 126. Chisholm's view is not representative of all proposition-theorists, some of whom deny that propositions are states of affairs to begin with.

[68] This instrumentalism in the idea of truth is found in James and especially in Dewey. But it even occurs in Peirce's version of pragmatism. Peirce says that the true opinion is the one on which all who investigate ultimately agree. (see C.S. Peirce, "How To Make Our Ideas Clear" in *Classic American Philosophers* ed. by Max H. Fisch (Englewood Cliffs, N.J: Prentice-Hall, Inc., 1951), 85-86. But since the investigators here are principally scientists who follow the method of hypothesis, it follows that the true opinion is the hypothesis that covers all the known facts and does so for an extended period of time. Such an hypothesis satisfies our goals as scientists and is to that extent true.

instead that P is true if and only if there is a correspondence between P and some simple fact in the world. That is still imprecise, if only because the correspondence in question must be specified. But it is narrow enough to count as a type of correspondence theory as opposed to a coherence, pragmatic or even a redundancy theory.[69]

Among correspondence theories, a plausible one construes the relation of truth-bearer and fact as one of similarity. Under this assay, when A says truly that John loves Mary, a relation of similarity obtains between the statement and the fact that John loves Mary. The ground of the similarity is that statement and fact share the selfsame state of affairs of John's loving Mary. It is one and the same state of affairs that is both expressed by A's sentence and exemplified in reality. It is just that it exists mind-dependently in the former and mind-independently in the latter. As content of a sentence, it depends on a stater; but as extra-linguistic fact it does not. This account of what it means to say that A's statement corresponds to a fact (and is hence true) is familiar and intelligible. The correspondence is nothing but an instance of the relation of similarity. The similarity here between statement and fact parallels other relations of similarity where the similarity implies a shared content or function.[70] John and Mary are similar in being human, 6 and 8 are similar in being divisible by 2, and so on. It would be awkward but one could say instead here, "John and Mary correspond to each other in being human" or "6 and 8 correspond to each other in being divisible by 2". The difference is only that in these latter cases none of the terms in the similarity relations are conventional signs. The similarity in these cases is non-symbolic as opposed to the symbolic similarity between A's statement and the fact in question.

But this account of the correspondence relation is unavailable to proposition-theorists. For the similarity in terms of which 'correspondence' is here construed implies that each term in the relation, i.e. truth-bearer and fact, is a complex of a state of affairs plus how it

---

[69] For a lucid account of the redundancy theory of truth see F.P. Ramsey, "Facts and Propositions" in *Truth*, ed. by G. Pitcher (Englewood Cliffs, N. J: Prentice-Hall, Inc., 1964), 16.

[70] Another account of similarity denies that the terms of that relation share a common content by virtue of which they are similar. Instead, the relation of similarity is construed as being ultimate and as not requiring a shared content as ground.

exists, i.e. as symbol in the statement and as symbolized in the fact. But under the proposition-theory it is this shared state of affairs in the two complexes and not either one of the complexes themselves that is true. It is the state of affairs itself or taken just as such that is true and not the complex of the state of affairs as stated, much less the complex of the state of affairs as existing in the fact. And it is this same state of affairs taken as such that proposition-theorists identify with propositions.

However, it seems that it is impossible both to identify truth-bearers with propositions in this sense and construe the correspondence relation in which proposition-theorists say truth consists as a similarity between two things that share a common state of affairs. Otherwise, since it is these very states of affairs that proposition-theorists call propositions, then the absurdity follows that the truth-relation is one in which proposition and fact share a common proposition.

To evade this and keep the idea that truth is the correspondence of truth-bearer to fact, proposition-theorists might construe the correspondence in question as identity and not similarity. A fact, they might say, is just another name for a true proposition. Truth-bearers conform to facts in that they *are* facts; they do not conform to facts in the sense of sharing a common content or state of affairs with facts. Truth, then, is not a relation of correspondence in the sense of a relation between two distinct things. To say that a proposition is true is not to say that it answers to some other thing, a fact. It is to say that the proposition is *itself* the fact.

However, identifying true propositions and facts commits a category mistake. When sub-classes belong to a wider class the former must be coordinate. Thus, sheep and wolves are meaningfully said to belong to the wider class *animal* because sheep and wolves are coordinate. But it is crossing categories to say that sheep and unicorns belong to the wider class *animal* since sheep are real while unicorns are fictional animals. In the first, both sub-classes have real being and so are coordinate. In the second, they are in-coordinate since one has but the other lacks real being. This clash of categories comes from equivocating on the class *animal*. In the second case but not in the first, 'animal' means two different things at once, namely, real animal and fictional animal. So it is no surprise that the sub-classes in the second division comprise an incongruous mix.

Identifying true propositions and facts makes the same error. Here, the two sub-classes that fall under the class *proposition* are facts (true propositions) and false propositions. But since facts and false propositions (objective falsehoods) have very different modes of being, this division too is crossed. It is evidently not the same sense of 'are' that is meant when it is said that facts *are* and that objective falsehoods *are*. Otherwise either falsehoods are just as real as facts or facts lose their ontological advantage over falsehoods. But as before, this conflict in status among the species implies ambiguity in the genus. The in-coordinate mix of species is due to equivocation on the genus *proposition*, just as in the previous case the incongruous mix of sheep and unicorns was due to equivocation in the wider set of *animal*. When facts are placed under the class *proposition* then the latter must have real being. No class that has real being such as a fact belongs to a wider class that has only objective being. Otherwise, since the former includes the latter the way that a species includes its genus, then the contradiction ensues that the class of facts has both real and objective being. But when the class of objective falsehoods is placed under the wider class of *proposition*, then the latter must have objective being only and not real being. And this for the same reason. To avoid incongruity, classes like objective falsehoods that have objective being only do not belong to a class that has real being.

It seems then that neither one of the two plausible accounts of correspondence in the correspondence view of truth are available to proposition-theorists. The similarity account implies that truth is a relation in which proposition and fact share a common proposition; and the identity account implies a category mistake. Proposition-theorists must therefore choose between the correspondence theory and their proposition-theory, but they cannot embrace both.

It follows that philosophers who want to keep the correspondence theory are better off identifying the bearer of truth with a statement. By 'statement' here it is not meant a sentence *type* since sentence types are sometimes used non-assertively. As Quine states, sentence-tokens, unlike sentence-types, are inherently pragmatic.[71]

---

[71] The inherently pragmatic function of sentence-tokens as truth-bearers is stressed by W.V. Quine in his *Philosophy of Logic* (Englewood Cliffs, N.J: Prentice-Hall, Inc., 1970, 14.

They are tied to a certain use. And the use they have when they are truth-bearers is to make an assertion. This they do by expressing a proposition. What is true, then, is the complex of a sentence-token together with the proposition it expresses. One might say that the former is the form and the latter the matter of a truth-bearer. Thus, truth-bearers are not propositions themselves but the sentence-tokens or linguistic complexes in which propositions figure. Unlike proposition theory, this makes it intelligible to say that truth-bearers and facts share a common content. And then what is meant by 'correspondence' in the correspondence theory of truth is easily explained as a relation of similarity between two complexes.

To this, proposition-theorists might retort that this implies that unless, say, someone says and judges that the earth is round then the earth's being round is not true. Therefore, truth is not a property of statements in the sense specified. But it is clear that this objection feeds on an ambiguity on the phrase, 'is not true'. True, that phrase is sometimes used non-intentionally to mean 'is not a fact'. And when it is used in this extended sense, then what it modifies is a state of affairs. In that case, the complex, *the earth's being round is not true* is equivalent to *the state of affairs of the earth's being round is not a fact*. But the phrase, 'is not true' is also used intentionally and straightforwardly to modify a statement, as in "George's statement is not true." When the phrase is used in the first sense, defenders of the view that statements in the sense specified are the bearers of 'true' fully agree with proposition-theorists that the implication is unacceptable. Few hold that facts owe their existence to the statements we make about them. But when the phrase is used in the second sense, i.e. to describe someone's statement, then, so far from it being absurd to say that when no one states that the earth is round then the earth's being round is not true, that implication is a perfect truism. For under this second sense of 'is not true', when no one states that the earth is round then there is no statement to that effect, and hence, *a fortiori*, no *true* statement to that effect.

Chapter Five
True Belief and Knowledge Revisited

The last three chapters dealt with truth and in particular i) the sense and types of truth, ii) how truth of any sort involves the idea of an end, and iii) the bearers of truth. This chapter concerns true belief and in particular its relation to knowledge.[72] It has three parts. I shows that two epistemic dicta, (1) and (2), imply skepticism. (1) is that the sense of a belief does not vary with its truth-value and (2) is that persons can come to know the very same thing that they once only truly believed. If these dicta are true then no one ever knows a fact. II argues that one answers the skepticism by distinguishing sense and referent in true belief that is not knowledge but identifying them in knowledge. But this answer calls for denying either (1) or (2). In III it is shown that it is (2) that must be dropped. Yet, (2) contains a kernel of truth. That is why it is mistaken for a truism to begin with. So while the letter of (2) is dispensed with, its spirit, what is called (2A), is retained. And unlike (2), (2A) accords with how, in II, the skepticism is answered.

I

In (1) 'sense' is synonymous with 'object' or 'content'. The sense, object or content of a belief is simply that which is believed by any person s when s has a belief. This might also be called a proposition, so long as it is not implied that propositions are self-subsistent entities existing independently of beliefs or facts. That a belief has a sense is shown by the fact that it is expressed in a sentence. And when it is, it is the sense of the belief that is so expressed. When I believe that Bill Clinton was a Rhodes scholar and say, 'Bill Clinton was a Rhodes scholar', what is expressed by this statement is not my act of believing but the sense or object of my belief. And that my belief has reference is shown by the fact that it is true. The same goes for

---

[72] Much of this chapter originally appeared in *Grazer Philosophische Studien*, vol. 52 – 1996/97, 127-135.

knowledge. When I express my knowledge that Bill Clinton is a Democrat by saying, 'Bill Clinton is a Democrat', what is expressed in this sentence is not my act of knowing but the sense or content of my knowing. And that that knowledge has reference is shown by the fact that knowledge entails truth.

In any case, let 'true belief' and 'truly believe' from here on refer to belief that is not knowledge as opposed to belief that is knowledge. Then, suppose I truly believe my wife is downstairs and continue to believe this, falsely, even later when she steps out into the garden. It seems evident that it is the very same thing (proposition) that is first truly and then falsely believed by me. And from this it follows that, if true beliefs have facts as their referents and if the sense of a false belief is evidently not a fact, then sense and referent are unidentical in a true belief. In any true belief, then, what is truly believed is the sense or content and not the referent of the belief.

As for (2), suppose that I believe on the basis of induction that the sum of any two consecutive numbers equals the difference between the squares of those numbers.[73] Suppose I come to this generalization by discovering by accident that it proves true in these three cases: 1 and 2 are three and the difference between the squares of 1 and 2 is 3; 3 and 4 are 7 and the difference between the squares of 3 and 4 is 7; 4 and 5 is 9 and the difference between the squares of 4 and 5 is 9. On the basis of these examples, I believe, but do not yet know, that the relationship will continue. But suppose I then apprehend the formula that, for any number n, $2n$ plus $1 = n$ plus 1 squared minus n-squared. As soon as I do, I go from merely truly believing that the relationship will continue to knowing that it will continue. Nor are instances of (2) only mathematical. Suppose I believe that my wife is calling to me from downstairs. I hear what I believe is her voice coming from the direction of the stairway. Suppose too that my wife and I are alone in the house and that no one else is even in the vicinity of the house. But since I do not know either one of these things, I cannot rule out the possibility that the voice I hear is that of

---

[73] I owe this example to Prof. R. S. Brumbaugh. See Stallknecht and Brumbaugh, *The Spirit of Western Philosophy*, David McKay Co., Inc. New York, 1964, p. 70-71.

my daughter. Then, as I move out of my study towards the stairway, the call not only gradually becomes louder, clearer and more recognizable, but I actually see my wife calling to me at the foot of the stairs. Here once again, I come to know the very same thing I previously did not strictly speaking know but only truly believed, namely, that my wife was calling to me from downstairs.

Assume, then, that (1) and (2) are true. To see how they imply skepticism, recall what is implied by (1). If (1) is true then, since facts are not the referents of false beliefs, then, (1a), there must be a dualism of sense and referent in any true belief. Further, (1b), what is truly believed by me when I believe something is the sense (content or object) and not the referent of the belief. Otherwise, since facts are the referents of true but not of false beliefs, it is not the same thing I believe when I first truly and then falsely believe P. In other words, if it is only assumed that facts are the referents of true but not of false beliefs, then the joint assertion of (1) and denial of either (1a) or (1b) is contradictory. But (1a), (1b) and (2) imply that sense and referent are distinct in true belief and knowledge both. This may be called the unidentity-thesis. In addition, they also imply that it is always senses of beliefs or propositions that are known by us and never facts. And this is skepticism. Thus,

(A)
(1a) Sense and referent differ in true belief.
(1b) What is believed in any true belief is the sense and not the referent of the belief.
(2) Persons can come to know the very same thing they once merely truly believed.
Therefore, (S), what are known are objective senses (propositions) *and not facts*.

II

The skepticism of (S) is answered by dropping the unidentity-thesis in favor of what may be called the identity-thesis. That is that sense and referent are the same in true belief and knowledge both. Under this move, the sense and referent of true belief and knowledge is a true proposition and a true proposition is just another name for a fact. The point is that if sense and referent are one in a true belief, then what I believe when I truly believe something is a fact. In that case, when I come to know the same thing I once only truly believed, what I come to know is also a fact. And then the skepticism in question is skirted. So defenders of this analysis, (B), can boast that the advantage of their view as over against the preceding one (A) is that (B) retains (1) and (2) *without* sacrificing knowledge of facts.

But the trouble with (B) is that it eliminates the difference between true and false beliefs. If sense and referent are the same in true belief and (1) is true then the sense of a false belief is a fact, just as it is in a true belief. To escape this, defenders of (B) might say that sense and referent are the same in true belief but not in false belief. When it is true, a belief has a fact as its sense but when it is false it evidently does not have a fact as its sense but something else, say, a false proposition. But aside from its arbitrariness, this escape succeeds only at the cost of denying (1). For under the escape, beliefs have a different sense or meaning depending on whether they are true or false. And so the challenge is, how is it possible to avoid the skepticism of (A), and at the same time retain both (1) and the difference between true and false belief? The dilemma here is one the second horn of which is itself a dilemma. The first horn of the main dilemma is skepticism and the second horn is the subsidiary dilemma of either denying (1) or assimilating false to true belief. Since the latter is a dilemma that confronts B, I use 'dilemma of (B)' from here on to refer to it and simply 'dilemma' to refer to the main dilemma.

A hint as to how to solve the dilemma comes from looking at what occasions it in the first place. As for the first horn, skepticism, it is evident that it grows out of the unidentity-thesis. If sense and referent are different in belief and knowledge and (1) and (2) are true, then when I come to know what I previously only truly believed, what I come to know is never a fact (the referent of the true belief and knowledge) but rather the sense of each one. And this is identical in each case. (1) and (2) are thus preserved at the cost of skepticism. And as for the second horn, i.e. the dilemma of (B), it is equally clear that it comes from the identity-thesis. If sense and referent are the same in both true belief and knowledge, then when I come to know what I previously only truly believed, what I come to know *is* a fact which is first believed and then known. Thus, (2) is retained and skepticism is avoided. But as was stated, if (1) is to be retained, then under this same identity-thesis a false belief *also* has a fact as its sense. So, to answer the skepticism in question, defenders of (B) or the identity-thesis must choose, unenviably, between abandoning (1) and assimilating false to true belief.

It seems, then, that to escape the dilemma, a third position, (C), must be taken as regards sense and referent in knowledge and belief. (C) denies that sense and referent are different in both belief and knowledge and also that they are the same in both belief and knowledge. For it is just these two extreme views that occasion the dilemma.

Alternatively, (C), distinguishes sense and referent in true and false belief but not in knowledge. It is thus a kind of synthesis of the identity-thesis at the one extreme and the unidentity-thesis at the other. Since it separates sense and referent in *both* true and false belief, (C) escapes the arbitrariness of (B) in this regard as well as the dilemma of (B). That is its advantage over (B). So if (C) answers the skepticism in question without the the arbitrariness and dilemma of (B), then (C) is to that extent preferable to (B). But (C) *does* answer that skepticism. Under (C), when I truly believe but do not know my wife is calling to me from downstairs, it is the sense or content of the belief that is believed by me. At the same time, the belief has a referent which is the fact itself that my wife is calling to me from downstairs. Sense and referent are thus distinct in the belief. But when I go from truly believing to knowing my wife is calling to me from downstairs, this dualism of sense and referent collapses. What in the previous true belief was the referent, i.e. the fact itself, now becomes the very sense or content of my knowing. Thus, the difference between true belief and knowledge is that sense and referent are identified in the latter but not in the former. Since under (C), therefore, it is facts themselves and not propositions that comprise the very sense or content of knowing, skepticism as regards facts is averted.

Moreover, that (C) preserves (1) is evident. When I continue to believe that my wife is calling to me from downstairs when actually she has stepped out into the garden, the sense or content of my belief remains unchanged even though the belief is now false. In other words, what I believe is the same thing even though, being false, the referent of the belief is no longer a fact. Thus, under (C), (1) is retained as well, and the meaning or sense of a belief does not vary with its truth-value.

But does (C) accommodate (2) as well? Here it will be objected by defenders of (A) or (B) that it does not. And then, when it comes to satisfying both (1) and (2), avoiding skepticism and keeping truth and falsity distinct, (C) holds no advantage over (A) and (B). The objection is that (2) goes unsatisfied under (C) just because in (C) it is propositions that are the objects of true belief and facts that are the objects of knowledge. But (2) specifies that it is the *very same* thing that it is first truly believed and then known by a person to be the case when a person moves from truly believing to knowing that something is the case.

There is but one other possibility and that is the converse of (C). It states, (D), that sense and referent are the same in belief but different in knowledge. Since, once again, it cannot be admitted that the referent of a false belief is a fact, followers of (D) must say that sense and referent are the same in *true* belief but different in false belief. But then, like (B), (D) appears to be arbitrary in this regard and, what is worse, implies that a belief means something different or has a different sense depending on whether it is true or false. And so (D), like (B), is incompatible with (1). Second, (D) also conflicts with (2). If what is truly believed is a fact but what is known is not, then it is not the very same thing that is first believed and then known when a person moves from true belief to knowledge. Third, (D) affirms rather than answers the skepticism in question. If it is not a fact but something else instead that is in or before my mind when I know something, then how are facts known by me? It seems, then, that since (D) retains the skepticism of (A) without satisfying either (1) or (2), then (D) is only a logical and not a real possibility.

(D) is also counterintuitive. If anything, it should be expected that sense and referent are the same in knowledge and different in belief. For it seems that knowing gives a degree of certitude that is often lacking in belief. But this is more consistent with identifying sense and referent in knowledge and differentiating them in mere true belief. For to say sense and referent are the same in a true belief is to say that a fact is the very content of such a belief, i.e. that it is a fact itself that is before or in the mind when something is believed. And to say that sense and referent are not the same in knowledge is to say, by contrast, that what is in or before the mind when something is known is not a fact but something else. But if so, then we should be surer in believing how things are than in knowing how they are.

It seems that we have reached an impasse. (A) both covers (1) and (2) and differentiates true and false belief. That is its strength. But its weakness is that it implies skepticism. Alternatively, (B) avoids the skepticism of (A) and also covers (2). But it does so at the expense of arbitrariness in regard to true and false belief on the matter of sense and referent. It does so also at the cost of the dilemma of (B). For its part, (C) covers (1) and avoids both skepticism and assimilating false to true belief. But for this it pays the price of giving up (2). And (D), the worst of all epistemological worlds, keeps the skepticism of (A) and the arbitrariness and dilemma of (B). And this it does without even the compensatory advantage of retaining (2).

What, then, can be done? How can (1) and (2) both be kept without either skepticism or assimilating false to true belief? The simple answer is that this is something that it is impossible to do. Either (1) or (2) are dropped or else either skepticism or eliminating the difference between true and false belief must be countenanced. Yet the curious thing is that (1) and (2) seem to be evident.

III

To solve the enigma, consider (2) more narrowly. (2) *appears* to be evident only because it is easily confused with another proposition, call it (2A), which *is* evident. Thus,

(2A) Persons can come to know what they once only truly believed.

It is easy to see how (2) is mistaken for (2A). But (2A) is weaker than (2), as genus is weaker than species. One cannot affirm (2) and deny (2A) any more than one can affirm that something is human and deny that it is an animal. But one *can* affirm (2A) and deny (2), just as one can affirm that something is animal and deny that it is human. Persons *can* come to know what they once only truly believed (2A), but from this it does not follow, (2), that it is the *very same thing* that is first truly believed and then known.

Substituting (2A) for (2) allows us to keep (C) without losing the kernel of truth in (2). For recall that the attraction of (C) is that it both answers the skepticism of (A) and avoids the dilemma of (B). Its only supposed drawback is its denial of (2). For under (C), it is not the very same thing that is first truly believed and then known since what is believed is not a fact and what is known is a fact. But if (2A) keeps what is wanted in (2) and if (2A) is satisfied by (C), then (C) becomes the only analysis that unobjectionably answers the skepticism.

To spell it out, despite their similarity, one consistently denies (2) and affirms (2A) just in case the word 'what' in (2A) refers to a *component* of the referent of the phrase 'the very same thing' in (2). Suppose that 'the very same thing' in (2) refers to a fact. And suppose that a fact is an existing state of affairs as opposed to, say, an imaginary state of affairs. In scholastic terms, facts are then a composite of essence and existence. Suppose even further that 'what' in (2A) refers to a sense or state of affairs just as such, taken apart from its existing. In that case, not only is the referent of 'what' in (2A) a component of (and hence unidentical with) the referent of 'the very same thing' in (2) but also, and because of that, the denial of (2) is compatible with the affirmation of (2A). Under (C), persons cannot come to know *the very same thing* they once truly believed, since, under (C), persons believe senses (propositions, states of affairs) and know facts. Nevertheless, persons can, under (C), come to know *what* they once truly believed. For what they believe, i.e. the sense or state of affairs taken apart from its existing, is a component of the fact which they come to know. The former is essence alone, as it were, while the latter is a composite of essence and existence both.

In other words, when I go from true belief to knowledge I *ipso facto* know what I previously believed just because the 'what' or object of my prior belief, i.e. a certain sense or state of affairs, is included in the fact I come to know. In knowing the composite I concomitantly know the simple, just as, in seeing an apple, I concomitantly see its redness. All the same, what I know is the fact itself and not just the sense, state of affairs or proposition in the fact, just as what I see is the apple itself and not just its redness. To borrow another scholastic contrast, the one is known or seen *per se* while the other is known or seen *per accidens*.

And so it can be said that, unlike (1) and (2), (1) and (2A) do not imply that facts are unknown to us provided only it is held, following (C), that sense and referent are the same in knowledge and different in belief. To hold, as in (A), that they are *different* in each (the unidentity-thesis) is to make the mistake of assimilating knowing to believing. That is why (A) implies skepticism. When knowledge is eliminated skepticism follows. On the other hand, to hold, as in (B), that they are the *same* in each (the identity-thesis) is to go to the opposite extreme of reducing belief to knowledge. That is why (B), unless revised, eliminates falsity. When belief is falsely assimilated to knowledge, all of us are infallible. The revision calls for making sense and referent the same in true belief but different in false belief. But the question of arbitrariness aside, this implies, as was said, that a belief means something different depending on whether it is true or false, in which case (1) is abandoned.

All of this (C) bypasses. For taking a middle path, (C) eschews the extremes of either making knowledge belief or making belief knowledge. And this it does by separating sense and referent in belief and identifying them in knowledge. This is how (C) gets between skepticism on the one hand and the dilemma of (B) on the other. True, (C) does this at the cost of giving up (2), but the loss of (2), we saw, does nothing to prevent our saying that persons sometimes come to know what they previously only truly believed (2A). And this is all that was ever wanted out of (2) in the first place.

To conclude, true belief is made knowledge just when the sense and referent of the belief become identified. For if sense and referent remain distinct in knowledge as they are in true belief that is not knowledge, then we are brought right back to (A). But then that same skepticism as regards facts breaks out all over again. This skepticism, moreover, is not evaded by identifying sense and referent in *both* true belief and knowledge. For to take this escape-route, (B), is to fall into the dilemma of (B), i.e. to get caught between assimilating false to true belief and saying that a belief means something different depending on whether it is true or false. Not only that, but (B) renders senseless the question of what converts mere true belief into knowledge. For as was shown, whereas (A) mistakes knowledge for mere true belief, (B) mistakes mere true belief for knowledge. If, under (B), mere true belief is in the first instance reduced to knowledge, then it is just for that reason futile to ask what it is that must be added to mere true belief to get knowledge.

Chapter Six
Mind and the Problem of Realism

It was argued in Chapter Four that the bearer of truth is identified not with judgments but with sentence-tokens or a certain use of sentences. Yet judgments and their analysis show how the problem of universals arises and how it is to be solved. As to the former, if one takes simple judgments like "Socrates is human" as signifying the exemplification of one kind of thing, i.e. a property by another kind of thing, i.e. a particular, then one invites the problem of universals. If Socrates exemplifies the universal humanity and universals are one, then how can Plato, Aristotle or anyone else also exemplify humanity? Nor does it help to construe exemplification as an external tie instead of an internal one. For then the particulars that exemplify universals are either bereft of properties altogether (i.e. are "bare" particulars) or else they are only copies of the properties they exemplify. Thus Socrates, according to Plato, is a mere copy of a human being. But in either case, no particular thing ever really is what it is said to be. As to the latter, one avoids the problem of universals without relinquishing saying what particular things really are by adopting the analysis of judgment that is proposed by Aquinas. That assay implies moderate realism as over against either extreme realism, nominalism or conceptualism on the status of universals.

To begin, the early Russell adopted what has been called the Realist Principle according to which primitive predicates occurring in simple true propositions denote real universals. Classic objections to this robust realism include a) how universals are predicated of many if they are by definition one and b) how that realism avoids types of infinite regress. Though these objections might suggest a turn to either nominalism or conceptualism, these latter positions are equally problematic. More promising is the moderate realism of Aquinas. By keeping straight the domains of the real and the logical, this moderate realism sidesteps both a) and b) without incurring the difficulties of either nominalism or conceptualism.

To unpack all this, I begin with defining the problem of realism. Then I show how mind and in particular judgment or predication can be brought to bear on the solution to the problem.

I

Realism in philosophy has at least three senses. There is realism as opposed to idealism, realism *versus* anti-realism and realism as over against nominalism.[74] Despite his critical idealism and anti-realism, Kant is a realist in the first sense. Otherwise his *ding an sich* is mind-dependent which it is not. And despite being an idealist in the first sense, Berkeley is a realist in the second sense. Unlike Locke and purposely opposing the latter's representationalist epistemology, Berkeley shuns making ideas as opposed to reality the objects of thought. True, what we directly know are ideas, says Berkeley, but the latter, says he, *are* reality and not, as with some of Locke's ideas, mental pictures or representations of reality.[75] Finally, despite rejecting realism of a Platonic stripe according to which there are self-subsistent Ideas or universals, Aquinas embraces both realism as opposed to idealism and realism as over against anti-realism.[76] St. Thomas never questioned either that things exist independently of our knowing them or that we can know these real things as they are and not just as constructed by us.[77]

These three realisms are related as follows: the first does not imply either the second or the third nor does the second imply the

---

[74] The word 'idealism' here is used to signify the view that what is is mind-dependent and not the view (such as Plato's) that there are timeless Ideas or Forms which are independent of minds.

[75] The difficulties of Locke's half-way house position that our ideas of primary qualities represent qualities in the object whereas our ideas of secondary qualities do not are of course as obvious as they are well-known, and Berkeley exposes all of these difficulties. See George Berkeley, *Three Dialogues between Hylas and Philonous*, R.M. Adams, editor (Indianapolis: Hackett Publishing Co., 1979. See especially the *First Dialogue*.

[76] Aquinas admits transcendent Ideas (i.e. his *universalia ante rem*) but so far from being self-subsistent, these Ideas exist in and depend on God's Mind.

[77] Realism in this sense does not of course imply that we can know everything there is to know about a thing.

third. But the second and third realisms do imply the first. If universals have ontological status apart from minds, then some things exist independently of minds. And if extra-mental things are the objects of thought, then some things are said to exist independently of minds.

In any case, rejecting both nominalism and conceptualism, the early Russell was a full-fledged realist. He adopted in his *Problems of Philosophy* what Alan Donagan has called the Realist Principle which he shared with G. E. Moore.[78] It states that primitive predicates occurring in simple true propositions denote real universals.[79] For true propositions of the form, say, a R b can be understood. But they cannot be understood unless R is understood. Moreover, some of these propositions correspond to facts or are true. Therefore, R denotes a real universal.

The robust realism implied by this argument has raised objections. Among the earliest appears in Plato's *Parmenides* (131) and *Philebus* (15b).[80] It was later aimed at hyper-realists like William of Champeaux by medieval scholastics of a more nominalist stripe. It is that if there are many particulars in which a universal is said to be present or as in this case many atomic facts of which the simple universal R is a constituent, then the contradiction follows that though in itself one, the universal becomes many. If being human is a universal and is in Socrates, then how can it be in Plato and Aristotle? If in what is expressed by the proposition "Jack is in his house", the universal *in* is one and is exemplified by Jack and his house, then how, in what is expressed by the proposition, "Jill is in her house" can the self-same universal be "divided from itself" and be exemplified somewhere else, i.e. by Jill and her house?

This problem for realists is posed not just by Plato himself in his *Parmenides* and *Philebus* and by Alan Donagan in his "Universals and Metaphysical Realism". It is also raised by Etienne Gilson in the

---

[78] Alan Donagan, "Universals and Metaphysical Realism" in M. Loux, ed., *Universals and Particulars* (Notre Dame, IN: University of Notre Dame Press, 1976), 130.

[79] Bertrand Russell, *The Problems of Philosophy* (London: Home University Library, Oxford University Press, 1912), 89-90.

[80] Plato, *Philebus*, in *The Dialogues of Plato*, translated by B. Jowett (London: Oxford University Press, 1953) Vol. III, 15b, 565-566. See also, *Parmenides*, vol. II, 131b, 674.

following imaginary exchange between Socrates and Aristotle.[81] Thus,

Socrates: "I should like to know, Aristotle, whether you really mean that there are certain forms of which individual beings partake, and from which they derive their names: that men, for instance, are men because they partake of the form and essence of man."

Aristotle: "Yes, Socrates, that is what I mean."

Socrates: "Then each individual partakes of the whole of the essence or else of part of the essence. Can there be any other mode of participation?"

Aristotle: There cannot be."

Socrates: Then do you think that the whole essence is one, and yet, being one, is in each one of the things?"

Aristotle: "Why not, Socrates?"

Socrates: "Because, one and the same thing will then at one and the same time exist as a whole in many separate individuals, and will therefore be in a state of separation from itself!"

Robust realists who cling to what Donagan calls Russell's Realist Principle might reply that this classic objection fails to spike either realism or the Principle. It only goes to show that universals, unlike the particulars that exemplify them, are not in space-time.[82] What is in space-time are particular instantiations of universals and it is these instantiations that are many while the timeless universal remains one. In terms of the example, it is two instantiations of the universal 'in' and not the universal 'in' itself that figures in the two atomic facts that Jack is in his house and that Jill is in her house. But then since each instantiation of a universal is particularized or glued to but one thing, realists are no longer saddled with the contradiction that universals are both one and yet multiplied in many. For it is the timeless universal itself that is one and it is its instantiations in space-time that are many.

Yet this way out spells ruin for robust or extreme realists. For they then abandon their core belief that two or more atomic facts such as Jack's being in his house and Jill's being in her house share

---

[81] Etienne Gilson, *Being and Some Philosophers* (Toronto: Pontifical Institute of Mediaeval Studies, 1952), 49.

[82] Alan Donagan, "Universals and Metaphysical Realism", in M. Loux, ed., *Universals and Particulars*, 134.

anything in common, in this case the relational universal 'in'. They cannot all include the universal since that is one and cannot be divided in many. Not just that, but if realists hold that such facts are spatial-temporal and nothing but the sum of their constituents, it becomes difficult to understand how the whole fact can be spatial-temporal when one of its parts (in this case the universal 'in') is not. Nor can these facts have in common any instantiation of a universal either, since these are unique and unrepeatable. We cannot even say that they are similar if by saying this it is meant that they all include the same universal. At best, we can say that they are similar *period*, i.e. that being similar is, in Quine's words, "ultimate and irreducible".[83] Though that might satisfy Quine, it cannot satisfy realists who insist that the facts that Jack is in his house and that Jill is in her house are similar by virtue of their somehow both including the universal 'in'. But the question remains, how can this be? How can the universal relation 'in', any more than any other universal, relational or qualitative, be one and yet divided in many?

Besides, positing universals as one sort of thing as over against particulars, another sort of thing, installs a hard and fast dualism. And that invites regresses not only of the Third Man type but also of the types alleged by Ryle and Bradley.[84] As to Ryle's, suppose that *a* exemplifies F and *b* exemplifies G where F and G are universals. Then these facts are instances of another universal, i.e. the relational universal of exemplification. Thus, we have, [(a exemplifies F) exemplifies E] and [(b exemplifies G) exemplifies E]. But now these two exemplifications of E exemplify a second-order universal of exemplification, E1, and so on, infinitely. The only way to stop this regress is to nip it in the bud and deny from the start that you need an extra thing called exemplification to tie *a* to F and *b* to G. But this move is unavailable to realists who would distinguish the two facts that *a* is F

---

[83] W.V. Quine, *From A Logical Point of View* (Cambridge: Harvard University Press, 1961), 10.

[84] I am indebted to Alan Donagan's discussion of these regresses in connection with realism. See Alan Donagan, "Universals and Metaphysical Realism" in M. Loux, ed., *Universals and Particulars*, 136–139. As to the Third Man regress in particular, see Gregory Vlastos, "The Third Man Argument in the *Parmenides*" in R.E. Allen, ed., *Studies in Plato's Metaphysics* (New York: The Humanities Press, 1965), 231–263. See also, P.T. Geach, "The Third Man Again" in R.E. Allen, ed., *Studies in Plato's Metaphysics*, 265–277.

and *a* is not F which hold at different times as follows: in the former, where the universal F is exemplified, there is a further relation of exemplification which ties *a* to F, whereas in the latter where F is not exemplified there is no further relation which ties *a* to F.

To make matters worse for robust realists, there is in addition Bradley's regress. Suppose the true statement, *a* R *b*, where R is a relation which ties *a* and *b*. To tie *a* and *b*, R must be linked to *a* by another relation, R1. But then another relation, R2, is needed to link *a* to R1, and so on to infinite regress, in which case *a* is never linked to R. A similar regress breaks out on the part of *a*. Since relations need terms to be relations and terms need relations to be terms, then in the fact *a* R *b*, *a* both conditions R and is conditioned by R. So within *a* are two aspects, namely, that whereby *a* conditions R and that whereby *a* is conditioned by R. Since these two aspects (call them alpha and beta) are related in *a*, then each one is both the condition of that relation and conditioned by it. That means that alpha for its part again harbors two aspects, i.e. that by which it is the condition of its relation to beta and that by which it is conditioned by its relation to beta, and so on endlessly. The same regress breaks out for monadic relations. If '*a* is green' is construed as '*a* exemplifies the universal green', where 'exemplifies' denotes the relational universal of exemplification, then to link *a* to exemplification, you need another relation, and to tie *a* to *that* relation, you need still another relation, and so on infinitely. So in view of all these problems, the question looms large as to whether robust realism and Russell's realist principle are really defensible, and if not, whether we are not better advised to abandon realism altogether and join the ranks of either nominalists or conceptualists on the issue of universals.

And yet, even if Russell's realism and his realist principle face daunting roadblocks, it hardly follows that *no* realism or realist principle can dodge those barriers. And if a case can be made for a more moderate realism which goes by a more modest realist principle, then going over to either nominalism or conceptualism would be premature. This is especially true since nominalists and conceptualists each have issues of their own. To allude to just a few, to meaningfully deny abstract ideas, nominalists must themselves have the idea of an abstract idea, and it is difficult to see how the idea of an abstract idea is anything but abstract. So having admitted one abstract idea, it seems arbitrary to exclude others. For their part, conceptualists admit abstract ideas but deny that they have any foundation in reality. That assumes that they know how reality is. Yet it is difficult to understand how they know this through any judgment, since judgment is through abstract ideas which they deny reflect reality. Besides, many conceptualists are anti-realists in the sense and to the extent that they hold that mind colors its objects. Now either mind itself is among the objects of mind or not. If not, then they admit an exception to their view. And since where there is one exception there might be others, then their conceptualism is compromised. But if mind *is* among the objects of mind then for all these conceptualists know, mind as it really is does not color its objects at all but is a passive *tabula rasa*.

That makes it all the more enticing to take a second look at the more moderate realism that was just mentioned, a version of which was held by St. Thomas Aquinas.[85] Aquinas had his own realist principle. It sides with Russell's in insisting that something in reality does correspond to a true judgment. But departing from Russell's, it denies that the correspondence is or need be one-to-one. For while knowledge implies an essential conformity of mind and object, the object's mode of being (*esse*) in mind differs from that which it has in things. Thus does this Thomistic unity-in-difference construal of correspondence reflect the essence-existence distinction. In any case, to bring out this moderate realism and show how it bypasses the ogre of universals being both one and divided in many, I consider concepts and predication.

II

Empiricists like Aristotle, Aquinas and Locke who admit universal concepts must answer this question: if we derive all our ideas from sense experience and the latter includes only particulars, then how do we acquire universal ideas? Their answer invokes the device of abstraction. Mind's powers include the act of focusing on what is common or at least what is similar among particulars and forming on its own a universal concept which includes those particulars in its

---

[85] St. Thomas Aquinas, *On Being and Essence* trans. by A. Maurer (Toronto: Pontifical Institute of Medieval Studies, 1949), Chapter III, 39-42.

extension.[86] In this case the universal concept is a species. A species is a general idea that has both intension and extension, the latter but not the former including the individuals that fall under that species. Thus, adverting just to the humanity of Sally, Sam and Sue without considering anything that uniquely belongs to any one of them, I form the general idea or species of being human. Included in the sense or intension of this species is being an animal and being rational but not being Sally, Sam or any other individual person. Instead, Sally, Sam and other persons comprise the extension or reach of the species. This is what is meant by saying that while a logical intention like a species does not include any individual in its sense or intension, it none the less does simultaneously implicitly include individuals in its reference or extension. Scholastic philosophers say that general ideas like this are products of what they call total abstraction.[87]

From total abstraction one distinguishes formal abstraction. Mind has the power of abstracting the form of a thing not only from individuals that exemplify that form but also from a certain composite of that form together with matter, say, the abstraction of humanity from Sue. Here, mind considers what it abstracts as impredicable of Sue. Extracting the part from any individual whole, mind cuts off that part from the whole for the sake of greater focus or analysis. The resulting concept, therefore, is not a species or logical universal by which we make judgments about various individuals. Instead, it is a kind of metaphysical universal which expresses a form as cause of an individual's participating in that form. Thus, I extract the idea of twoness from two sparrows or the notion of circularity

---

[86] For example, see John Locke, *An Essay Concerning Human Understanding*, A.S. Pringle-Pattison, ed., (Oxford: The Clarendon Press, 1960), Book II, chapter XI, no. 9, 10, 88-90.

[87] The distinction of total and formal abstraction in Aquinas occurs in *Summa theologiae* I. 85, 1 *ad* 1 and in *In Librum Boethii de Trinitate*, V, 3, *Resp*. For the classic commentary on St. Thomas's distinction see Cajetan, *Commentary on Being and Essence*, trans. by Kendzierski and Wade (Milwaukee: Marquette University Press, 1964), Question I, 45-47. See also, J. Maritain, *Philosophy of Nature* (New York: Philosophical Library, 1951), 15-23; A. Maurer, *St. Thomas Aquinas: The Division and Methods of the Sciences* (Toronto: The Pontifical Institute of Medieval Studies, 1953) xxiv-xxv, nn. 29, 30. Whereas Maurer holds that there is a difference between St. Thomas and Cajetan on the distinction, Maritain contends that the difference between them is purely verbal.

from a brazen disc.[88] And here it is understood that the sparrows are two and the disc circular by virtue of twoness and circularity, respectively. Signifying only a part of their subjects, these non-logical concepts are therefore impredicable of those subjects. No one says that the brazen disc is circularity or that the sparrows are twoness.

Besides shunning the predication of parts of wholes, a successful assay of predication also avoids saying that the real is either the logical or the psychological. Just as Sally is not her humanity, so too is she not the idea of human either in the logical or in the psychological sense of 'idea'. These two senses of 'idea' Aquinas distinguishes in his analogy of a statue.[89] We might use The Concord *Minuteman*. That memorial has its own identity and individuality as a statue. It is of a certain material, weight and dimensions, stands beside The Old North Bridge in Concord, MA., and so on. From this standpoint, it is self-enclosed or non-intentional. But the Concord *Minuteman* can also be viewed as intentional, i.e. as representing any and every minuteman who served in the colonial militia. In this sense it is not individual but universal, i.e. one with respect to many. Similarly, taken as an event in my mind, my idea of human is unique and individual. It belongs only to me. But taken logically or as a species, my idea of human is not individual but universal i.e. something that has both extension and intension and through which I predicate one thing of many. Like the *Minuteman*, then, my idea of *human* can be viewed either as individual or as universal, either as self-enclosed or as extending to many. From the former standpoint the idea is psychological only, but from the latter it is logical.

However, it is evident that it is not as having either one of these modes that we predicate *human* of Socrates, Plato, or any other person. Even though we use the species-concept *human* to predicate being human of Socrates, it is not that concept but being human just as such that we predicate of him. Further, even though my idea human is a psychological act or event which is uniquely mine, it is not

---

[88] By formal abstraction form or act is abstracted from matter or potentiality in such a way as to exclude the latter from the former. For that reason, the product of this abstraction is impredicable. Otherwise a part is predicated of a whole.

[89] St. Thomas Aquinas, *On Being and Essence*, trans. A. Maurer, chap. III, 41-42.

the idea human in this sense of 'idea' either that is predicated of Socrates or any other person.

If the first is true, then the following pseudo-syllogism ensues: Socrates is human, human is a species, and therefore Socrates is a species.[90] The absurd conclusion unmasks the ambiguous middle term. What is said of Socrates in the first premise is being human taken in itself apart from individual or universal existence. Here, the word 'human' is used to refer to the essence human. However, the word 'human' in the second premise is used to refer to the concept human, i.e. to human as it exists as a species or logical intention in the mind. The pseudo-syllogism thus confuses that which (*id quod*) is predicated with that by which (*id a quo*) it is predicated which corresponds to confusing use and mention.

If the second is true, then another pseudo-syllogism follows. For if Socrates is human and human is a psychological event, then Socrates is a psychological event. And once again, the senseless conclusion comes from equivocating on the middle term. What is said of Socrates in the first premise is being human taken apart from any mode of being, individual or universal, while 'human' in the second premise signifies one among many unique psychological acts or events.

One must sidestep all of these pitfalls. If the *human* that is said of Socrates expresses that by which he is human to the exclusion of anything else that belongs to him, then the whole Socrates is said to be one of his parts. It would be like saying that a circular saw is it circularity. If the *human* that is said of Socrates includes the individuality of Socrates, then either *human* is impredicable of Plato or else Plato is one with Socrates. Finally, if the *human* that is said of Socrates is the idea *human* either as logical species or as psychological event, then the real Socrates is said to be either the logical species *human* or a psychological event.

Aquinas strove to bypass all of the above blind alleys of predication through the concept of existential neutrality.[91] The latter has in different ways and for different reasons surfaced in other philosophers. Recall Meinong's ploy of positing non-existent objects that are neutral between being physical and mental in part to make sense

---

[90] —, *On Being and Essence*, trans., by A. Maurer, chap. III, 42.
[91] —, *On Being and Essence*, trans. by A. Maurer, ch. II–III, 35–42.

of denying that things like golden mountains exist.[92] Again there is Bolzano's identification of the bearer of truth with a *satz an sich*, the proposition in itself, which is neutral between physical and mental existence.[93] Third and closer to home, there is James' neutral monism under which the real is neutral as between the physical and the mental. That allows one and the same real thing to occur in two different contexts at once. Thus, it is one and the same neutral book which I perceive and which is on the table. It is just that it occurs in different contexts while being in itself neither physical nor mental. This proved to be attractive to James because it seemed to avoid both representationalism and idealism. Under this neutralism, I can say that I perceive the real book and not just my own idea or copy of it. And I can say this without identifying the real book with the idea of it. By analogy, James gives the example of paint which in a pot in a paint shop is saleable matter but which on canvas has a spiritual function. It is made at once material and spiritual by addition, though in itself and apart from the addition it is neither one.[94]

All of this aside, existential neutrality in Aquinas' theory of predication comes to this: that in order to predicate P of S what P denotes must be taken as indifferent to existence. The essence *human* exists either particularly *in re* or universally *in mente*. But in order to say that Socrates is human what the predicate 'human' signifies can have neither one of these modes of existence. For one thing, particulars are impredicable. For another, if 'human' here signifies Socrates' humanity, then 'human' cannot be said of Plato or of Aristotle. And if it is the universal concept 'human' that is predicated of Socrates, then Socrates is said to be a universal concept. For if Socrates is human and what is here predicated of him is the universal 'human' then it follows that Socrates is a universal.[95] Yet we do truly say that Socrates is human. How is that possible?

---

[92] Meinong, A. "Uber Gegenstands Theorie", in Gesammmelte Abhandlungen II, 483-486.

[93] Bernard Bolzano, *Wissenschateslehre*, no. 19.

[94] William James, "Does 'Consciousness Exist"? in Bruce Wilshire, ed., *William James: The Essential Writings* (Albany: State University of New York Press, 1984), 165-66.

[95] St. Thomas Aquinas, *On Being and Essence*, trans. by A. Maurer, chap. III, p. 42.

Aquinas answers that it is possible because predicates are existentially neutral. If the property of being human were not indifferent to the particular existence it has in Socrates, then it could not be said of any other human. For to be human would then to be Socrates. But in point of fact it is so predicated. And if that same essence human were not indifferent to the kind of universal existence it takes on in the intellect as a result of being known *via* the universal concept 'human', then it could not be said of any human being at all, Socrates included. Otherwise any particular human is said to be a universal concept. The human that is predicated of Socrates is therefore the essence *human* taken as existentially neutral, i.e. considered apart from either particular or universal existence. Otherwise it is impossible to cover the fact of predication and in this case saying that Socrates is human.

Just as the 'human' predicated of Socrates is neither particular nor universal, so too is it neither numerically one nor numerically many. If the former, then there could not be many humans, but if the latter, then being human could never be numerically one. But the fact of the matter is that human is numerically many in Socrates, Plato and Aristotle and numerically one in Socrates. Therefore the 'human' said of Socrates is entirely neutral as between being either numerically one or numerically many. And so it is that behind judgment and hence logic is the ontological paradox that what we say things are in and through predicate terms is in itself existentially neutral.[96] That sounds contradictory unless we heed Aristotle's idea that being is said in many senses, and in this case those senses are being in the sense of essence and being in the sense of existence.

Nevertheless, the numerical many-ness of humanity in Socrates, Plato and Aristotle does not exclude humanity's also being one in these and all other persons. It all depends on what you mean by 'one'.

---

[96] Aquinas notes that both Averroes and Avicenna shared this idea of the existential neutrality of essences. It is fair to say that Aquinas was influenced in this view both by these Arabic philosophers and by Aristotle. See St. Thomas Aquinas, *On Being and Essence*, trans. by A. Maurer, chap. III, p. 41. For an insightful discussion of essences and existential neutrality, see E. Gilson, *Being and Some Philosophers* (Toronto: Pontifical Institute of Medieval Studies, 1952), chap. III, p. 75ff.

To spell it out, humanity's being either numerically one or many is consequent on its being quantified just as humanity's being a genus or a species is consequent on its being known. What are numerically one or many are individual humans or horses and not humanity or horseness itself taken apart from existing in individuals as spatial objects or in minds as universal concepts. There is an analogy in arithmetic. What are numerically one or many are not twoness or threeness taken as such but individual two's and three's. True, these are not in physical space like individual humans and horses but they are nonetheless in what might be called intelligible space.[97] Here the quantity is not physical but intelligible. When we put planks together to make a shed, we acknowledge that the result, i.e. the shed, is larger than any one of the planks. Similarly, when we add five ones together to make five, we say that the result, i.e. five, is larger than any one of the ones. The evident difference is that in the former "larger than" refers to physical space or physical quantity whereas in the latter "larger than" refers to mathematical space or intelligible quantity.

And yet, the numerically many and similar humanities in Socrates, Plato and Aristotle are nonetheless one or undivided *in definition*, just as in arithmetic the ones I add up, though five in number, are one or undivided in definition. Here, oneness or unity follows on being in the sense of quiddity or objective sense. It is the unity behind definition and not a quantitative unity. What is numerically divided might be in definition undivided. For whether humanity exists intentionally in minds or really in Socrates or other persons, it is in each one of these modes or conditions one and the same in objective sense. Otherwise internal division breaks out in the very definition of 'human'. And since genus and difference comprise the definition, that amounts to saying that either the genus or the difference is split. If the latter, then 'human' is defined as a rational or a non-rational animal. The *differentia* here having been lost by the divisive disjunct, "rational or non-rational", 'human' then covers brutes as well as ourselves. If the former, then 'human' is defined as a rational animal or non-animal. The proximate genus here having been compromised by the divisive disjunct, "animal or non-animal", 'human'

---

[97] Wittgenstein speaks of still another kind of space which he calls logical space. See L. Wittgenstein, *Tractatus Logico-Philosophicus* 1.13, p. 7; 2.11, p 15.

then covers rational pure spirits as well as ourselves. In either case, since either being rational or being an animal ends up being accidental to a human being, this conceptual rift in the definition of 'human' obliterates its determinate sense.

So despite the fact that there are as many humanities as there are individual persons, they all of them have the same definition. And to the extent that this definition is one with respect to many, it is universal. And this universality or oneness in definition that belongs to the many similar humanities exists quite independently of minds. Thus, it is this simultaneous unity in sense or definition that it has alongside of its numerical many-ness that allows us to say compatibly (if paradoxically) that in Socrates, Plato, Aristotle, etc. humanity is many and particular even as it is one and universal. When in these individuals it is being in the sense of quantity that is concerned, humanity is many in all three. But when it is being in the sense of essence or definition that is concerned, humanity is one for all three.

III

What with these distinctions and to return to the problem of realism, is it not also through this idea of existentially neutral essences that Aquinas avoids that contradiction which the robust realisms of William of Champeaux in the Eleventh Century and of Russell and Moore in the Twentieth Century straightaway imply, namely — and in the somber words of the *Parmenides* — that a universal is "really divisible and yet remains one"? For in the view of Aquinas, though something does correspond to 'human' in the true statements, "Socrates is human" and "Plato is human", yet it is not, as robust realists say, the existent universal human or primitive existent universals into which 'human' is analyzed. That is to assume that the correspondence of the real and the logical must be exactly one-to-one. It is to think that because some essence is numerically one in mind or logic, that it is therefore in that way one in things. But in assuming this isomorphism, robust realists make the mistake of foisting the rational onto the real. For it is only in mind and as a result of being known that any essence takes on the logical property of being a one with respect to many. In other words, what in reality answers to the true statements "Socrates is human" and "Plato is human" is not an existent universal corresponding one-to-one to the universal concept 'human', but rather the essence human. Taken in and of itself, this essence is neither numerically one (as for instance it is in Socrates) nor a logical one with respect to many (as for instance is the species 'human'). For that reason it can perfectly consistently be said to be multiplied in many humans.

What with recognizing the existential neutrality of essences, then, can it be said that Aquinas gets to have his philosophical cake and to eat it too? Lacking numerical oneness in the first instance, such essences can be said to be multiplied in many without contradiction. And thus is the similarity of the many grounded. But by the same token, the dreaded contradiction is not dodged by hypostatizing timeless independent universals as over against temporal particulars. That escape both denies the commonness among facts upon which Russell rightly insisted and spawns those celebrated regresses which have driven philosophers from realism altogether.

To further specify Aquinas' move, in reality no essence stands abstracted from individuals and yet related to them as one with respect to or as predicable of many. This logical relation of one to many any essence acquires only as a result of its being in mind as, say, a genus or a species.[98] It is we who make it a one with respect to or as predicable of many. In this it is analogous to the *Concord Minuteman* which we saw is simultaneously both really and logically one. It is really one in number (as opposed to the many statues in the British Museum) and logically one with respect to all colonial soldiers just because we make it so.

Yet though this logical one-to-many relation which characterizes, say, the species *human* that is now in my mind is numerically or existentially one concept, nevertheless the one which enters into that relation and which is predicable of many humans is an essential and not an existential oneness. Otherwise it could not be so predicated. If the *human* that is predicated of Socrates is numerically one

---

[98] St. Thomas Aquinas, *On Being and Essence*, trans. by A. Maurer, chap. III, p. 41. For an excellent analysis of universality in the thought of Aquinas and how it consists in a relation to many, see R.W. Schmidt, *The Domain of the Logical According to Saint Thomas Aquinas* (The Hague: Martinus Nijhoff, 1966), pp. 188-201. For a lucid and penetrating discussion of this logical one-to-many relation in logic see H.B. Veatch, *Intentional Logic* (New Haven: Yale University Press, 1952), 22-27;105-115.

then either it could not be said of Plato and Aristotle or else Plato and Aristotle are one with Socrates. Moreover, that this same predicated *human* is an essential one and not an existential or numerical one is shown by the fact that numerically or existentially many humans such as Socrates, Plato, Aristotle, etc., all have one and the same definition, and essence is what a definition signifies. In fact, saying that being human is existentially one in Socrates and existentially many in Socrates, Plato and Aristotle makes sense only if this essential oneness is presupposed, i.e. only if it is (essentially) one and the same thing that is said to be both existentially one (in Socrates) and existentially many (in Socrates, Plato and Aristotle).

Nor can it be doubted that this move from robust to moderate realism reaps the added advantage of blocking those intractable regresses which were previously mentioned. Such regresses are nothing but fading phantoms when universals are excluded in the first place as real entities alongside of particulars. The classical Third Man regress takes hold only when things of one sort, particulars, are said to be similar by virtue of their exemplifying a thing of another sort, a universal. And the Rylean and Bradleian regresses get started only if it is assumed from the start that you need the extra relation of exemplification to tie, say, the universal 'in' in the fact that Jill is in her house to Jill and her house. But if under the measured realism of thinkers like Aristotle and Aquinas it is denied from the start that universals are things alongside of the things we call particulars, then all these regresses are cut off at the pass. They are reduced to prodigies or pseudo-puzzles of our own making. In philosophy as in life, self-made problems often block our way.

And so it seems that what proved to be a fatal stumbling block for robust realism i.e. how existent universals can be both one and yet divided in many, fails to appear under the moderate realism and the more modest realist principle of a thinker like St. Thomas who saw himself in this regard as a true follower of Aristotle. It fails to surface just because these philosophers deny that the correspondence of logic and the world is isomorphic, an assumption which wrongly foists the logical onto the real. For both philosophers always insisted that the domains of logic and reality be kept perfectly straight and sound. Only then should we bypass either patterning the real after the rational or the rational after the real.

Chapter Seven
Logic and the Mind-Body Issue

The last chapter addressed the problem of universals in relation to judgment or predication. In essence it argued that Aquinas' analysis of simple judgments like "Socrates is human" solves the problem of universals by implying moderate as opposed to extreme realism on the status of properties. Since the *human* that is said of Socrates is in itself neither numerically one nor many, nothing prevents its being said of either many or of one person. And since it is in itself neither universal nor particular, nothing prevents its being said of either a particular human like Socrates or of several humans like Socrates, Plato and Zeno.

But the theory of predication bears upon other metaphysical issues too one of which is the issue of body and mind[99]. Common answers to that puzzle include identity materialism, dualism, idealism and epiphenomenalism. Yet it seems that all four of these accounts of a person contradict basic logic and in particular the predicable relations of genus, species and difference. And metaphysical theories grow suspect to the extent that they flout ordinary logic and language. That suggests another answer which accords with those relations. This is the kind of double-aspect theory known as hylomorphism as applied to human beings. On the negative side, this alternative opposes hypostasizing either mind or body. Under it what is called the human mind is not a substance in its own right. Nor is the human body another kind of substance cut off from mind. Both are false abstractions. On the positive side, it holds that mind and body are different effects of two sides or aspects of the same thing. These more basic principles of a person are the form and matter of a

---

[99] Part of this chapter appeared in my Introduction to Scholastic Philosophy (Lanham, Md: University Press of America, 2013), Chapter Five

person. From the union of both in a human being issue the effects of mind and body.

To spell it out, genus and difference in logic answer to and so reflect not things but the material and formal sides of things, respectively. So as regards a human being the difference rational is taken from and signifies not a substance in its own right or a thing called mind but the form of a substance which is the source of mental activities. By the same token, the genus animal is taken from and signifies not a substance in its own right or a complete thing called an animal body but the matter of a substance.[100] And this when specified by the form to which the difference rational answers makes for a human substance. So corresponding to the subject-term in the judgment say, "Socrates is a rational animal" is neither a mind-substance, an opposed body-substance, nor indeed two such substances. Instead there is a two-in-one, i.e. a single substance comprised of two opposed aspects which fit together hand in glove. These are matter and form which the genus and the difference in the foregoing judgment respectively reflect.

Thus our ordinary logic mirrors a hylomorphic view of persons which gets behind the notions of mind and body and of which these notions are false abstractions. That is one stage of the argument. A second comes from examining not what the predicables of genus and difference answer to in the real world i.e. the material and formal sides of a thing, respectively, but what they are in and of themselves. They are of course logical relations and as such issue from our rational side. Moreover, as relations they imply and depend on both a subject and a term. As to the latter, a genus is the genus *of* something, i.e. a species and a difference is the difference *of* something, i.e. a genus. As to the former, the relating of a difference to its genus or of a species to its genus is something that necessarily takes place in a subject, namely us. Relations of any sort are accidents and hence imply a subject. But in this case the nature of these logical relations shows that their subject cannot be any one of the things that the four answers to the mind-body issue say a person is. How these predicable relations exclude the four common answers that were mentioned follows upon a close analysis of these relations.

---

[100] St. Thomas Aquinas, *On Being and Essence*, trans. A. Maurer (Toronto: Pontifical Institute of Medieval Studies, 1949), chapter II, 35–36.

I

The predicables are relations. As an employer is necessarily the employer of an employee and a sibling by definition is the sibling of a sister or brother, so too is a genus necessarily the genus of a species, a difference the difference of a genus and a species necessarily the species of individuals. It is also evident that these predicables are logical and not real relations. For they are subjects or predicates of judgments and no whole that is logical can be composed of parts that are real. Though the facts to which true judgments correspond are real beings, the judgments by which one signifies those facts are beings of reason. In no real whole does one of its parts stand apart from it. Nor is that part at the same time referred back to the whole. Yet in judgments predicates both stand apart from their subjects and yet refer back to those subjects.[101] This simultaneous analysis and synthesis is all the work of reason. Thus, in judging that whales are mammals, one uses the genus-concept *mammal* as a mental device to predicate the real character of being a mammal of the thing signified by the species-concept, *whale*. Similarly, in judging that Willy is a whale, one uses the species-concept *whale* as a logical tool to predicate the real nature of being a whale of the individual named by the subject, "Willy".

Though they are similar to classes in some ways, predicables are not classes. Like classes, genera and species are non-physical. A class is no more a group of physical things, like a group of flying geese, than is a genus or a species. Nor is a class a transcendent or subsistent entity like a Platonic Form. For suppose that the class of humans is such a timeless thing. Then so too are its members. For the members of a class are not outside that class but belong to it. And it is difficult to see how either real individuals or ideas of them, both of which are temporal, can possibly belong to or be members of some timeless thing. The only way to avoid this is to posit timeless indi-

---

[101] How in judgment the predicate both analyses the subject and is united to it Aquinas explains. See for example, St. Thomas Aquinas, *Summa theologica*, A. Pegis, ed. (New York: The Modern Library, 1948) I, Q. 85, a. 5, reply to obj. 3415-416. For a detailed account of these functions of judgment, see H. B. Veatch, *Intentional Logic* (New Haven: Yale University Press, 1952), 164-69. See also, R.W. Schmidt, *The Domain of Logic According to Saint Thomas Aquinas* (The Hague: Martinus Nijhoff, 1966), 209-212.

vidual humans as members of the timeless class of humans. But then, unbelievably, we all of us have a twin in a Platonic heaven. So it seems best to say that like genera and species classes or sets are mental or logical constructions.

Yet predicables and classes are not different names for the same thing. For one thing, though there are null-classes like the class of mermaids, the idea of a null-species is a contradiction in terms. That is because species are logical (as opposed to grammatical) predicates and logical predicates must be the predicates of logical subjects. But nothing without reference is the logical subject of a judgment. Therefore, since species are predicates of logical subjects and the latter have reference, it follows that the idea of a null-species is self-contradictory. For another, a species refers some property to an individual. Thus, the species *whale* in "Willy is a whale" applies the property of being a whale to the subject, *Willy*.[102] So in any predication by species, the predicate signifies a real part of the subject. However, though having a common property G is the foundation of several individuals belonging to the same class C, the latter is not a predicate. C in no sense applies or assigns G to a subject. Instead, this lowest-level class C is simply a group which we construct (i.e. a logical construct) in which we include those individuals which we take to be G.

This intentionality of a species i.e. its having the character of referring some property to a subject not only marks it off from a class but also shows how it is a predicable. When you judge that Willy is a whale, you abstract the property of being a whale both from Willy and from every other whale. For if the individuality of Willy is included in the sense of the predicate *whale*, then you evidently cannot predicate whale of Wally or of any other whale. You can predicate the property of being a whale of any and every individual whale just because you explicitly include none of these individuals in that predicate.

Yet to predicate being a whale of Willy, Wally or any other whale, one must not abstract whale from those individuals to the point of cutting it off from them entirely. Abstraction is not preci-

---

[102] Aquinas affirms this basic intentionality of predicates in knowledge. See St. Thomas Aquinas, *Summa theologica* I, q85, a5. See also *Summa theologica* I, q84, a2 and I, q85, a2.

sion.¹⁰³ This happens when, say, on considers whaleness as a real part of, say, Willy, i.e. as something in Willy that is set off from Willy's individuality or that other part of Willy which makes him Willy. Considered as a part in this way, whaleness is evidently impredicable of any individual whale. No one says that any real whole (in this case Willy) is one of its parts.

So to predicate whale of Willy one must get between including Willy in the sense of the predicate and entirely excluding Willy from it. For the first implies that whale, if predicable at all, is predicable of Willy only; and the second implies that whale is impredicable of any individual whale, since no whole is said to be one of its parts.

Passing between the horns of this dilemma is just what a species or any other predicable does. This they do by having both intension (sense) and extension. This allows the synthesis that *whale* both includes and excludes Willy. It includes Willy in its extension but excludes Willy from its intension. One predicates whale of Willy, Wally, etc. because the species *whale* by which one does this lacks the individuality of any one whale in its sense. This is what is meant by abstraction. Yet one does this without judging or saying that a whole is one of its parts because this abstraction is not a precision. That means that, as a species, *whale* in the judgment, "Willy is a whale" signifies the whole and not just a part of the subject Willy. And that is because, though it excludes the individuality of Willy or any other whale from its sense or intention, the species *whale* nonetheless includes those individuals in its extension. Thus does one predicate a whole of a whole and not a part of a whole when one judges that Willy is a whale.¹⁰⁴

This feature of implicit inclusion in logic parallels the presence of potentiality in things. Individuals with some properties are never absolutely cut off from other properties but implicitly or potentially contain them. A green leaf in summer is potentially brown. Though not actually brown, it is not absolutely cut off from brown. Open to brown, the leaf can be said to be an open thing. Similarly, though the

---

¹⁰³ For an account of the difference between abstraction and precision and of how the former allows whereas the latter excludes predication, see St. Thomas Aquinas, *On Being and Essence*, trans. A. Maurer (Toronto: Pontifical Institute of Medieval Studies, 1949), chapter II, 33–38.

¹⁰⁴ St. Thomas Aquinas, *On Being and Essence*, trans. A. Maurer, chapter II, 33–38.

species *whale* no more explicitly includes Willy than the green leaf actually includes brown, it is no more absolutely cut off from Willy than the green leaf is absolutely cut off from brown. Instead, it implicitly includes Willy as the green leaf potentially includes brown. Thus is it an open concept, as the leaf is an open thing. By contrast, real greenness is never open to being brownness and so is a closed thing. Recall Plato's comment in the *Phaedo* that of two opposed forms "...one of them can never become the other"[105] Correspondingly, since, as a part of Willy, whaleness is impredicable of him, then the concept *whaleness* is a closed and not (like the species *whale*) an open concept. The difference is that whereas in reality it is properties which are latent in individuals, in logic it is individuals that are latent in known properties (species). Those stark dualisms that characterize some metaphysics find no place either in logic or reality.

II

Though properties are latent in real individuals and individuals are latent in species in the senses specified, the terms of this latent-relation are distinct in each case. *One* thing is said to be latent in *another*. Individuals are not their properties nor are species the individuals they intend. If it is wrong to infer separateness from distinctness (an error, as was just implied, that is behind most hard and fast dualisms in philosophy), then it is equally wrong to infer sameness from non-separateness. You cannot infer that A and B are the same just because they are not separate. Otherwise size and shape are the same because they are inseparable.

This is true in the case of body and mind. Suppose that some philosophers hold that body and mind are distinct. From this they would wrongly infer that they are separate things. Similarly, suppose that they deny that body and mind are separate things. From this they would wrongly infer that they are the same. Just because body and mind are not separate substances, it hardly follows that they are names for the same thing. Between dualism and identity materialism lie other options.

---

[105] Plato, *Phaedo*, in B. Jowett, trans., *The Dialogues of Plato* (Oxford: The Clarendon Press, 1953) 103b 5, 461.

Of these, the true one is implied by the logical relations of genus, difference and species which have just been reviewed. Recall that a predicable is a relation of both analysis and synthesis in which some feature of a thing is both abstracted from it and united to it. In judging that Willy is a whale, one pulls out the property of being a whale from Willy by analysis and simultaneously reunite it to Willy by synthesis. A sign of the first is the distinction of subject and predicate, while the sign of the second is the copula 'is' by which one reunites the abstracted predicate from the subject. So the relation of species is a logical device of both analysis and synthesis. And as it is with species, so is it with genus and difference.

These logical relations are nowhere found in a body. You will never find in the brain the logical relation in which a property is both abstracted from an individual and yet referred back to it as is the case in a judgment by species. Relations in a body like the brain are relations between particular parts of that body and not between a particular part and some abstracted property. Thus, in this particular tree are spatial relations between the tree's parts. These hold between particulars such as one branch and another, one leaf and others, etc. There is not in addition a relation between one of these particular parts and some abstracted property that of the tree. True, some brain-event or state might correspond to this logical relation of species to individual. But it can never *be* that relation. Nothing in the brain is an abstracted property which is nonetheless linked to the individual from which it is abstracted. That being the case, the logical relations of genus, difference and species imply that the one who makes those relations is identified neither with her body nor with one or more parts or events in her body. Under identity materialism, no account of these predicable relations is therefore possible.

Moreover, consideration of the predicables also defeats the very opposite view, idealism. Under it, persons are identified with immaterial individual minds. Their bodies are therefore accidental to them. To see how the predicable relations exclude idealism too, recall that a species includes a genus in its sense but not *vice versa*. Hence, the species includes something that is not included in the genus. This is the difference which lay outside the genus. Thus, the species larch includes the genus tree but not *vice versa*. Otherwise all trees are larches. So in addition to the genus tree, the species larch includes some difference which is outside the genus. Similarly, the species human includes both a genus and a difference.

Now among genera, some are wider than others. The genus plant is wider than the genus tree. That implies that there is a widest genus. Otherwise no genus has determinate sense. If the genus plant is wider than the genus tree and the genus organism is wider than the genus plant, and another genus is still wider than the genus organism, and so on, *ad infinitum* – so that there is no widest genus – then, since any one genus (say, tree) includes an infinite number of wider genera, then no one genus has fixed sense.[106] But since that is false, then there is a widest genus which all the others include. If it is then assumed that *genera* signify some element in things,[107] then every individual thing in the world includes what the widest genus signifies.[108]

But to continue, this referent of the widest or simple genus does not have the nature or character of being immaterial. Otherwise, since every species includes both its proximate and remote genera (as tree includes plant, organism, etc., all the way to the widest genus), then there are no such things as bodies. But since that is unbelievable, then it follows that to the extent that they include genera all the way up to the widest genus, all species (and hence the species *human*) include a material element. But since species are predicated of individuals, then persons are no more identified with their minds than they are with their bodies. To the extent that it re-

---

[106] The widest genus is simple and not a composite of genus and difference or else it is not the widest genus. Compare Wittgenstein's argument that there must be simple objects if factual propositions are to have precise sense. See L. Wittgenstein, *Tractatus Logico-Philosophicus,* trans. Pears and McGuinness (London: Routledge & Kegan Paul,1961), 2.02-2.0211. For a lucid discussion and interpretation of Wittgenstein's argument, see David Pears, *The False Prison: A Study of the Development of Wittgenstein's Mind* (Oxford: The Clarendon Press, 1987), chapter 4. See also, David Pears, *Ludwig Wittgenstein* (New York: The Viking Press, 1970), 57-65.

[107] This realist assumption as regards the predicables is justified in section III below.

[108] For Aquinas and the scholastics, the referent of this widest genus (i.e. the idea *substance*) is primal matter or matter that in itself is without form, just as the widest genus is genus without difference. If it is assumed, then, that logic reflects reality, then the necessity of a widest genus in logic is an argument for positing primal matter in metaphysics.

flects hylomorphism, therefore, the logic of genus, difference and species, then, defeats idealism no less than identity materialism.

Furthermore, the predicable relations eliminate dualism too. This might appear surprising if not contradictory. For it was just argued that those relations imply that persons have both a material and an immaterial side and dualists hold that a person's material body is different from her immaterial mind. So if that is their claim and if the predicable relations imply that persons in fact include a material as well as an immaterial side, then how is dualism *falsified* by those relations?

The answer takes two steps. The first is to grasp the relation between genus and difference in any composite concept. The second is to see how that logical relation mirrors a real relation. As to the first, the relation in question is one of the conceptually unsaturated to what saturates it, i.e. of the logically unspecified to what specifies it. Thus, in the composite idea *organism*, the genus is the open or unsaturated concept *body* which is closed, filled or saturated by the difference-concept *living*. As Aquinas notes, the genus *body* signifies something which has a form through which three dimensions characterize it, leaving it open exactly what that form is.[109] For that reason, the difference *living* is implicitly contained in the genus *body*. In other words, the relation between genus and difference is that of the logically open and implicit to what closes that openness and makes that implicitness explicit.

As to the second, this logical relation of the open to what closes it mirrors and is based on the real relation of the potential to what actuates it or of matter to form. The logical relation between the genus *body* and the difference *living* answers to the real relation of potency to act or of matter to form in the thing signified by the idea *organism*. In reality something can have a form through which three dimensions can characterize it *no matter what that form is*, i.e. whether it is non-living or living. Reflecting this real openness is a corresponding logical openness. For the genus *body* is susceptible of various *differentiae* through which the idea of having three dimensions can be realized. Genus is to difference in our ideas what matter (potentiality) is to form (actuality) in things. Genus, difference and spe-

---

[109] St. Thomas Aquinas, *On Being and Essence*, trans. A. Maurer, chapter II, 33-34.

cies in our concepts, says Aquinas, answer to matter, form and composite, respectively, in the world.[110]

But this implies that the predicable relations falsify dualism too. Assume that our concepts of things generally include a genus and a difference which reflect the real relation in those things of matter (the potential) to form (the actual) respectively. Then it is wrong to say with dualists like Descartes that a person is composed of two distinct things or substances, i.e. a mind-substance and a body-substance. Instead, like everything else in the world, a person is one thing or substance with the distinct aspects of the potential and the actual or of matter and form. No separate substance in its own right, what we call mind or intellect is the effect of the formal or actual side of a substance, say, a person's soul. And no separate thing that stands starkly opposed to another thing, i.e. a mind-substance, the human body results from the union of the formal-side and the material-side of one and the same substance, say the person Socrates. For this is just what the predicable concept *human* signifies. The latter, like all our ideas of things in the world, is composed of genus and difference. But so far from its being isolated or cut off from the difference, the genus implicitly contains the difference as that through which it can be realized. And together they comprise the species. If, then, logic maps the world,[111] then what the logical two-in-one or species *human* signifies is a real two-in-one, i.e. the human essence in which matter and form or the potential and the actual fit together as tongue in groove.

Finally, the predicable relations falsify epiphenomenlism no less than identity materialism, idealism and dualism. Unlike Platonists and idealists and like Aristotelians and identity materialists, epiphenomenalists hold that being a body enters into the definition of a person. A person is no disembodied soul but a certain kind of animal. Yet epiphenomenalists recognize that persons differ from other animals by exemplifying abstract reasoning which in their view is distinct from and irreducible to matter. And in this they depart from identity materialists. This distinctly human thought or reasoning is in their view due to the size or structure of the human brain. They do

---

[110] St. Thomas Aquinas, *On Being and Essence*, trans. A. Maurer, chapter II, 35-36.

[111] This assumption is defended in section III of this paper.

not deny that non-human animals think but they hold that, due to their smaller or less intricate brains, non-human animals think on a lower level than humans.

Moreover, in common with dualists, epiphenomenalists hold that the mental is irreducible to the physical. Yet departing from dualists, they insist that mental events entirely supervene on the body or bodily events. Mental events or activities could not exist unless there were certain bodily states or events which lay behind and cause them. However, though some mental events might cause others, no mental event can ever cause a bodily event. The causality works only from the physical to the mental or from the mental to the mental but never from the mental to the physical. So epiphenomenalists would hold that though mental, the predicable relations of which we speak, i.e. genus, difference and species are all of them ultimately caused by certain physical states or events in the brain or nervous system.

But it is difficult to see how this could ever be the case. For recall that in any one of the predicable relations, the predicate both pulls some property out of the subject and refers it back to the subject. We saw that the distinction of subject and predicate in a judgment and their unification by the copula 'is' signify this analysis and synthesis, respectively.

But how can epiphenomenalists any more than identity materialists admit this analysis and synthesis in judgment? To be reunited to the subject by an act of mental synthesis that is signified by the copula, the property signified by the predicate must have been abstracted from it by a prior act of abstractive analysis. That means that in judging that Willy is a whale, one possesses the abstract concept of being a whale. Now if the task for identity materialists is to show how an abstract concept can possibly be located in a body, the task for epiphenomenalists is to show how either the body, which is particular and concrete, or some state or event in the body, which is also particular and concrete, can possibly produce what is not particular but what is the very opposite, i.e. universal and abstract. If it causes or produces anything at all, one particular thing or event can only cause or produce another particular thing or event. It follows that epiphenomenalism is no more compatible with the fact of predication than are either identity materialism, idealism or dualism.

III

Nevertheless, it will be objected that the argument that predication excludes dualism and idealism in particular rests on an undefended realism. For the case assumes that genus, difference and species answer to something in reality. This presumed realism opposes both nominalism and conceptualism. For under both it is denied that logical devices like the predicables answer to anything in the world. So to show that predication clashes with idealism and dualism, this objection must be met.

Aside from the arguments which were proffered in the previous chapter, one can support realism as regards the predicables by exposing the flaws in both nominalism and conceptualism. Nominalists deny abstract ideas altogether, genera and differentiae included. And though conceptualists admit abstract ideas like genera and differentiae, they deny that they answer to anything in reality. On the contrary, reason creates them out of itself for its own purposes. Accordingly, genus, difference, and species signify appearance and not reality, i.e. how we either conveniently or innately construe the given and not how things really are. In the scientific revolution which came with Galileo, a quantitative view of the world replaced Aristotle's qualitative one. Under this change, only those features are real which are measurable. The rest supervene on the measurable together with perceiving subjects and belong to appearance. Based on quality and not quantity, then, genus, difference, and species just reflect the way we human beings view or organize reality and not reality itself. But if so, then from the genus-difference schema in logic one falsely infers the matter-form complex in reality.

This harbors a kernel of truth. And that is that classification, along with the predicables of genus, difference and species that figure in it, are in fact the work of reason. Like concepts and syllogisms, they are not real beings but that type of *entia rationis* which some scholastics called second intentions. Yet it hardly follows from this that conceptualism is true and that these second intentions lack any foundation in reality. Not just that, but it seems that conceptualism of the modern Kantian type self-destructs.[112] If under this tran-

---

[112] I distinguish modern or Kantian conceptualism which is otherwise known as anti-realism from medieval conceptualism. Following Kant's "Coper-

scendental turn mind colors its objects then when mind's object is mind, then it follows that mind colors mind. That means that in "Mind colors its objects" the subject-term 'Mind' can only refer to phenomenal and not to real mind. But then Kantian-inspired conceptualists cannot say after all that mind really does color its objects. For all they know, real (as opposed to phenomenal) mind does not color its objects but is a *tabula rasa*, knowing things as they are. And then their message comes to nothing.

Nor can they even say in the first place that in "Mind colors its objects" 'mind' refers to phenomenal mind. For what in their view colors its objects is knowing or subjective mind and not known or objective mind or as Kant put it, the transcendental as opposed to the empirical ego. But having no empirical content, subjective or transcendental mind does not belong to phenomena at all. So the irony is that under the slogan of modern conceptualism, i.e. "Mind colors its objects" 'Mind' has no suitable referent. It can refer to neither mind in itself or mind as known, i.e. to neither real mind nor phenomenal mind. It follows that in the axiom of modern conceptualism i.e. "Mind colors its objects" no referent can be assigned to the subject-tem 'Mind'.

To answer this, conceptualists might concede that the judgment, "Mind colors its objects" is unmeaning. All intelligible judgments are about phenomena. However, so far from being phenomenal, mind is instead (along with things-in-themselves) the condition of the phenomenal. And what is a condition of the phenomenal does not itself belong to the phenomenal without implying that something is the condition of itself.

Yet this reply is unavailable to our conceptualists. If, instead of belonging to phenomena, mind is the condition of it, then mind is unknowable. But in that case Kantian-inspired conceptualism collapses. As N.P. Stallknecht once put it,

> ....Once we call mind unknowable, along with the thing-in-itself, we must admit that space, time, and the categories need no longer be recognized as necessary characters of our mode of awareness, for we cannot determine what is neces-

nican revolution" the former but not the latter takes the transcendental turn in philosophy.

sary to something unknowable. And with that admission Kant's system crumbles.[113]

As for nominalism, it seems that it too self-destructs but in a more obvious way. The concept of an abstract idea figures in the nominalist disclaimer, "There are no abstract ideas". Yet that concept is neither a sense image nor a copy of one. It is not particular or concrete but universal and abstract. Thus in denying abstract ideas nominalists admit at least one abstract idea namely, the idea of an abstract idea. They must then find a way of dissenting from abstract ideas without denying that there are abstract ideas. But this proves to be an impossible task. For just as believing that P implies judging that P, so too does disbelieving that P imply denying that P.

But if in the ways indicated nominalism and conceptualism are self-destructive then does not that constitute an indirect argument for realism? And if so, then does not the realist assumption behind our argument against dualism and idealism appear to be justified after all by the troubles which nominalism and conceptualism each incur by their own anti-realistic assays of the predicables?

---

[113] N.P. Stallknecht and R. Brumbaugh, *The Spirit of Western Philosophy* (New York: David McKay Co., Inc., 1964), 381.

Chapter Eight
The Paradox of the Soul

The last chapter showed how the logical theory of the predicables excludes identity materialism, standard dualism, idealism and epiphenomenalism as regards the metaphysical issue of mind and body. Yet the question remains as to whether the hylomorphic assay of persons which that theory implies is compatible with religion and in particular Christianity[114]. For is the view that the human soul is the substantial form of the body compatible with the Christian belief that the human soul survives death? How can the form of any body survive the corruption of that body when the latter consists in the separation of form from matter and on Aristotelian principles form depends on matter? This is especially a problem for a philosopher like Aquinas who is both an Aristotelian and a Christian. In any case, an immediate reply would urge that the question is from the start nonsensical if corruption is defined as the separation of a thing's form from its matter. For the soul is not to begin with a thing but the form of a thing, and nothing is separated from itself.

Nevertheless, though Aquinas would make this reply, he would concede that it is not enough to ensure the soul's survival. For he held that even though it is nonsense for the reason just given to say that the forms of other living bodies, say trees, corrupt, he would none the less concede that these forms do in a sense corrupt when the bodies of which they are forms corrupt. They corrupt *per accidens* and not *per se*. So if the form of a tree corrupts *per accidens* due to the *per se* corruption of the tree whose form it is, then why not say that the form of a human being, i.e. its soul corrupts *per accidens* due to the *per se* corruption of the person whose form or soul it is?

It seems that Aquinas has an answer to this and that his answer turns on working two distinctions together, i.e. that between the

---

[114] Part of this chapter appeared in my Introduction to Scholastic Philosophy (Lanham, Md: University Press of America, 2013), Chapter Five

soul's essence and its existence and that between the soul's essence and its power. For its essence or definition the soul depends on matter since the soul is defined as the form of the body. But for its act of existence the soul does not depend on matter. This is shown by the soul's power of understanding which Aquinas holds is independent of a bodily organ. And a thing's mode of existence is known by its power. Yet this seems to split persons in two. Under it matter enters into the definition of a person's essence but not into the definition of a person's existence. And if in the philosophy of Aquinas essence follows existence (and not the other way around) this would seem to invite the charge that Aquinas in the end reverts to Platonism on the matter of the soul's essence. Aquinas can only answer this by distinguishing two ways in which concepts depends on matter, i.e. intrinsically and extrinsically. The latter allows the soul's existential independence of matter without reverting to Platonism on the matter of the soul's essence.

In any case, the issue of the compatibility of the soul's being both form of the body and existentially independent of the body I address last. But first I show how Aquinas defends the two theses that feed the paradox, i.e. that the soul is form of the body and yet that it is existentially independent of the body.

I

The strongest argument for the latter, states Aquinas in *On Being and Essence*, is the soul's power of understanding. Forms, he there says, are understood or are actually intelligible only when "they are separated from matter and material conditions".[115] By 'matter' here it is meant prime matter and by 'material conditions' it is meant the conditions of concreteness and individuality. This separation occurs only through the power of an intelligent substance. When, for example, we know some form F, F extends to or is predicable of many particulars. But if in such knowledge F is received in our intellects as in matter, then F would be restricted to but one particular thing. For matter limits any form F to this or that F. Hence, our knowing F is not a

---

[115] St. Thomas Aquinas, *On Being and Essence*, trans. by A. Maurer (Toronto: Pontifical Institute of Medieval Studies, 1949), chap. IV, 43.

case of F's being received in a material passivity.[116] The fact that the forms we know extend to or are predicable of various individuals is incompatible with their being received in our intellects as in matter. In other words, the character of universality or of being predicable of many that forms have as a result of their being in the passive intellect is inconsistent with a form's being in matter. Aquinas's argument is conveniently outlined as follows:

1 We understand some form F if and only if F is actually and not just potentially intelligible.

2 F is actually intelligible if and only if F is the form of the passive intellect.

3 It is a condition of F's being the form of the passive intellect that F is separated from matter and material conditions.

4 Hence, we understand some form F if and only if (i) F is the form of the passive intellect and (ii) F is to that extent separated from matter and material conditions.

5 If our passive intellect is either a body or the form of a body, then it is not the case both that F is the form of the passive intellect and that F is separated from matter and material conditions.

6 But it is evident that we do understand some form F.

7 Therefore, the passive intellect is neither a body nor the form of a body.

As for 1 and 2, intellect goes from potentially knowing F to actually knowing F and this implies that, with respect to F, intellect is passive.[117] This passivity of intellect with respect to F consists in its capacity to receive or be actualized by F. Just as in natural change matter receives or is actualized by form, so in knowing does the passive intellect receive or come to be actualized by form. In each case is the potentiality in question, i.e. matter and passive intellect, formless. As matter in natural change is pure potentiality for form, so in noetic change is intellect a blank tablet "on which nothing is written".[118]

---

[116] St. Thomas Aquinas, *Summa theologica* in A. Pegis, ed., *Introduction to St. Thomas Aquinas* (New York: The Modern Library, 1948) I, Q. 84, a. 2, 381-82.

[117] ———, *Summa theologica* in A. Pegis, ed., I, Q. 79, a. 2, 339.

[118] ———, *Summa theologica* in A. Pegis, ed., I, Q. 79, a. 2, 339.

Yet the two potentialities differ. Otherwise either matter is cognizant of the forms it receives or the possible intellect is not cognizant of the forms it receives. Says Aquinas,

> Then, too, prime matter is not cognizant of the forms which it receives. If, then, the receptivity of the possible intellect were the same as that of prime matter, the cognizant intellect would not be cognizant of the forms received. And this is false.[119]

This leads us to 3. When matter is actualized by the form F, the result is an F-thing, something that is naturally or physically F. But when the passive intellect receives the form F, no such result occurs. The passive intellect does not become an F-thing in receiving or in being actualized by the form F. Thus, when matter receives the form of feline, the result is a feline thing, i.e. a particular cat. For matter to receive the form of feline is for a particular cat to come to be. But when the passive intellect receives or is actualized by the form of feline, no particular cat is produced. The passive intellect does not become a cat in knowing what a cat is in and through receiving the form of feline. Nor, for its part, does matter know what a cat is in and through receiving the form of feline. Contrasting the receptivity of matter with that of both sense and intellect on this score Aquinas writes:

> Now, immutation is of two kinds, one natural, the other spiritual. Natural immutation takes place when the form of that which causes the immutation is received, according to its natural being, into the thing immuted, as heat is received into the thing heated. But spiritual immutation takes place when the form of what causes the immutation is received, according to a spiritual mode of being, into the thing immuted, as the form of color is received into the pupil which does not thereby become colored.[120]

What is meant by saying that F is received in matter according to a natural mode of being while F is received in both sense and intel-

---

[119] ——, *Summa contra gentiles*, trans. J. F. Anderson (Garden City, N.Y.: Doubleday & Co.,1957) Bk II, chap. 59, 5, 178.
[120] ——, *Summa theologica* in A. Pegis ed., I, Q. 78, art. 3, 328–29.

lect according to a spiritual mode of being? Aquinas's answer is that 'receiving a form F according to a spiritual mode of being' has two senses. Either F is received as separated from both matter and material conditions or F is received as separated from matter but not from material conditions.

Sense knowledge receives its forms spiritually in the second sense while intellectual knowledge receives its form spiritually in the first sense. Because the sense of sight does not physically become green in receiving the particular green it sees, it is not a material potentiality or matter. Green here is not received in matter. That is what is meant by saying that it receives green as separated from matter. This is the second sense of receiving a form spiritually. In this same sense, the sense powers of animals as well as humans receive forms spiritually. Even so, the sense of sight does not receive green apart from material conditions. For the green it receives is always concrete and particular and never abstract and universal. And since concreteness and particularity are due to matter which limits any form F to this or that instance of F, it follows that green as well as all other sense objects are not received apart from material conditions, even though they are received apart from matter. That is why the sense powers do not receive their objects spiritually in the first sense.

Like the sense powers, the passive intellect too does not physically become the form it receives. My intellect does not become a cat in knowing cat any more than my sense of sight becomes green in seeing green. Forms are no more received in matter when they are received in intellect than they are received in matter when they are received in sense. But unlike the sense of sight and all other senses, the intellect receives its forms apart from material conditions in addition to receiving them apart from matter. Otherwise the objects of intellect would, like the objects of sense, be particular and concrete. But as it is, they are the very opposite. What I understand is understood universally and abstractly. Therefore, it can be said (as in 3 above) that it is a condition of my passive intellect's receiving some form F that F is separated both from matter and from material conditions.

That elicits two questions. First, what explains the fact that sense powers receive their objects spiritually in the second sense? Second, what explains the fact that the intellectual power receives its forms spiritually in the first sense? That takes us to 5.

As for the first question, Aquinas answers that the explanation of this is that the sense power is neither prime matter nor a body. Otherwise in sense knowledge the various sense powers would physically become the forms which they receive. Yet, because sense objects are always received under material conditions (i.e. are concrete and particular) their respective sense powers, though neither matter nor a body, are nonetheless intimately connected with a body. For any sense power is the very form or act of a bodily organ. Sight, for example, is the form of the eye. It is this close association of sight with the eye that explains the concreteness and particularity that characterizes the objects of sight. The same goes for the other senses.

That suggests the answer to the second question. For Aquinas infers from this that since the objects of the intellectual power are not concrete and particular but abstract and universal instead, then that power is not the form of a bodily organ. In that sense is it a separated power, i.e. separate from a bodily organ. Spelled out the argument is this: If a cognitive power is the form of an organ, then the objects of that power are concrete and particular. But the objects of understanding are not concrete and particular but abstract and universal. It follows that the intellectual power in us is neither a body nor even the form or act of a body.[121]

To summarize the argument, the species of things are known only if "the intellect in act and the intelligible in act are one",[122] i.e. only if it is those species themselves and not some copy of them are in the intellect. But a condition of a species being in the passive intellect is that it be abstracted from matter and material conditions. For things are received according to the mode of the receiver, and the intellect receives things abstractly. But it is in turn a condition of this abstract mode of reception that the passive intellect is immaterial. It follows that the species of things are known only if the passive intellect is immaterial.[123]

---

[121] ——, *Summa theologica* in A. Pegis, ed., I, Q. 85, a. 1, 401–02.
[122] ——, *Summa contra gentiles*, trans. J. F. Anderson, Book II, chap. 59, 13, 180. See also Aristotle, *De anima*, III, 4 (430a 3).
[123] ——, *Summa contra gentiles*, trans. J. F. Anderson, Book II, chap. 50, 3, 149.

So it is in the view of Aquinas that any object of knowledge is proportionate to its power.[124] The more dependent a power is on matter the more dependent on matter is its object. In the order of being, a power's status determines the status of its objects. Therefore, in the order of knowledge, one can deduce the status of a power from the status of its objects. Since, then, i) sense objects are individual while the objects of intellect are universal and ii) matter is the principle of individuality, then the sense power must be more dependent on the body than the intellectual power. But since for the reasons given, forms are not in *either* power received in matter, some other difference between the two powers as regards their relation to matter explains the difference between their respective objects. That difference in the view of Aquinas, is that a sense power, though not a body, is none the less the act of a bodily organ, whereas the intellectual power is neither a body nor even the act of a bodily organ.

II

That the intellectual power is not the act of an organ does not imply that the soul whose power it is is not the form of the body. Otherwise it is assumed that a soul has the same status in relation to matter as does its distinctive power. But that not only is not obvious but it is also untrue. The soul, says Aquinas, *is* the form of the body even though, paradoxically, its intellectual power is not the form of a bodily organ.

For this hylomorphic assay of soul and body, Aquinas gives indirect proofs. If Socrates is composed of soul and body as two complete substances, then Socrates is a mere aggregate and not unqualifiedly speaking one.[125] Not just that, but if what unites these two substances is another substance, then a further link is required to link the latter to what it links, and so on, *ad infinitum*?[126] To avoid all this, one might, with Plato, identify Socrates with his intellectual soul. That implies that Socrates' body is accidental to Socrates. But in that case, propositions like "Humans are animals" and "Humans are sen-

[124] ——, Summa theologica in A. Pegis, ed., I, Q. 85, a. 1, 401–02.
[125] ——, Summa contra gentiles, trans. J.F. Anderson, Book II, chap. 57, 3, 169.
[126] ——, Summa contra gentiles trans. J.F. Anderson, Book II, chap. 58, 8, 175.

tient beings" are accidental and not essential predications.[127] Besides, if Socrates' body is accidental to Socrates and no one senses without a body, then it is not one and the same person, Socrates, who is conscious both that he understands and that he senses.[128]

Of the direct proofs, one turns on the idea that difference is derived from the form.[129] To spell it out, though the intellect is not a body, body is nonetheless essential to what a person is. For the definition of a human being includes animal and the definition of animal includes body. If body is accidental to a person, then animal is not the genus of human.[130] But the definition of a human being includes rational as well as animal. For the distinctive, fundamental operation of a species is not accidental to it but belongs to its definition, and understanding is the distinctive, fundamental operation of humans. If understanding is accidental to a person, then rational is not the *differentia* of human. So the principle of understanding in humans, i.e. the intellectual soul, is part of what it is to be human. But it is evidently not the part from which genus is taken. For genus is taken from matter and we saw that something excludes matter to the extent that it is intellectual. Unlike genus, difference or distinctiveness comes not from matter but from form.[131] It follows that the intellectual soul in a person is related to that person as his or her substantial form.

A second turns on the idea that a body is living by virtue of being *such* a body and not by virtue of being a body.[132] Otherwise all bodies are alive. But that a body is such a body is due to its form and not to its matter. Otherwise, since all bodies are composed of matter, all bodies are of the same sort. And then the very idea of being such a body as opposed to being another body is senseless. But the soul is defined as that by virtue of which a body is such a body, i.e. a living body. It follows that the soul is the form of any living body and hence the form of the human body.

---

[127] ——, *Summa contra gentiles*, trans. J.F. Anderson, Book II, chap. 58, 7, 175.
[128] ——, *Summa theologica* in A. Pegis, ed., I, Q. 76, a. 1, 293-96.
[129] ——, *Summa theologica* in A. Pegis, ed., I, Q. 76, a. 1, 293-96.
[130] ——, *Summa theologica* in A. Pegis, ed., I, Q. 76, a. 3, 303-06.
[131] ——, *On Being and Essence*, trans. A. Maurer, chap. 2, 33.
[132] ——, *Summa theologica* in A. Pegis, ed., I, Q. 75, a. 1, 281-82.

III

Having reviewed what occasions the paradox, I return to the paradox itself. Does Aquinas recognize the enigma of saying that the soul is both form of the body and independent of the body? And if he does, does he try to show how those two theses are, and can be seen to be, compatible?

That St. Thomas recognizes the paradox is shown by his raising the objection that the soul's status as form of the body is incompatible with the immateriality of the soul's intellectual operation and power. But, so the objection runs, since the latter has already been shown, it follows that the soul is not the form of the body. Thus,

> Again, a thing's having its being in common with a body must have its operation in common with a body, for every thing acts in keeping with its being. Nor can the operative power of a thing be superior to its essence, since power is consequent upon principles of the essence of a thing. Now, if an intellectual substance is the form of a body, its being must be common to it and the body.... Therefore, an intellectual substance not only will have its operation in common with the body, but also its power will be a power in a body – a conclusion evidently impossible in the light of what has already been said.[133]

This objection (call it O) is conveniently summarized as follows:
(O)

1 Suppose that the soul is the form of the body.
2 Then the soul's being is common to it and the body.
3 But the operative powers of a thing follow its being.
4 So the soul's operative powers are common to it and the body.
5 But if so, then the soul's operative powers are in the body.
6 But it has been shown that the intellectual power of the
  soul is not in the body.
7 Therefore, 1 is false and the soul is not the form of the body.

---

[133] ——, *Summa contra gentiles* trans. J.F. Anderson, Book II, chap. 56, 18, 168.

To answer this objection is to explain the paradox in question. It is to show how the soul can be both the form of the body and yet independent of the body. Going by Aristotle's principle that activity follows being, Aquinas holds that we can infer how something is (exists) from knowing how its activity is. So if intellectual activity is intrinsically independent of matter then so too is the intellectual soul which is the subject of that activity. But at least simple apprehension of the forms of material things is an intellectual activity that is intrinsically independent of the body. It follows that the passive intellect which is actuated by those same forms is also intrinsically independent of matter.

At *Summa contra gentiles*, chap. 69, 5-6, Aquinas fields the objection by denying the assumption on which it feeds. And that is that every power is consequent upon essence. In terms of (O), Aquinas denies that 2 follows from 1. He would also deny that (O)3 is necessarily true. If (O)3 is false then (O)7 is compromised and (O) fails. 'Being' in (O)3 (as in (O)1) has the sense of essence. Yet, a soul's operative power need not follow the soul's being in the sense of its essence. It might follow its being in the sense of its existence. What (O)3 states, then, is not necessarily true of all powers of the soul. This reply hangs on Aquinas' celebrated distinction of essence and existence. It also turns on distinguishing the power of the soul from its essence, with the result that the former need not follow the latter.

What with these distinctions in place, (O) goes by the board. For then it does not follow, as (O) assumes, that *every* power of the soul is common to it and the body just because the soul's essence, as form of the body, is common to the soul and the body. For some powers might follow on the soul's existence and not its essence. And these powers would escape being in the body just in case the soul's existence is independent of the body. But that the soul's existence *is* independent of the body is shown by the fact that understanding is, for the reasons given, separate both from matter and material conditions. Since that implies that the intellectual power is not in a body and since any power that comes from the soul's essence *is* in a body (since body is included in the species human) it follows that the intellectual power is consequent on the soul's existence and not its essence. Thus,

Concerning the fifth argument, let it be said that because the soul is in its substance (essence) the form of the body, it does not follow that every operation of the soul must be performed by means of the body, so that every power of the soul will be the act of a bodily thing.... (the soul) can produce an operation without the body, as being operationally independent of the body; since it is neither *existentially* dependent on the body.[134]

Nevertheless, it might be objected that this Thomistic compromise fractures souls, splitting them in two. It is as if the soul's essence goes one way and its existence goes another. Souls depend on matter for their essence but not for their existence. True, drawing this distinction *prima facie* skirts the contradiction that souls in the same respect both do and do not depend on matter. But does it really escape the contradiction? If matter enters into a thing's definition, then is it possible that that same thing exists independently of matter? Is that not like saying that though the concept *animal* enters into the concept *dog*, there can nonetheless be non-animal dogs?

This last question Aquinas would answer in the negative. True, if a predicate P enters as a constituent part of the definition of a subject S, it is impossible that S exists without P. Therefore, since matter or body enters as a constituent part into the definition of a person, it follows that no person ever is or exists without a body.

Even so, what holds for persons need not hold for the souls of persons. And eschewing Platonism, Aquinas denies that persons are identified with their souls. True, persons can neither be defined nor can they exist without matter. In this they are just like anything else whose essence is a composite of matter and form. With respect to all such things, one cannot say that their existence runs contrary to their concepts. If their concepts or essences include matter as a constituent part, then there is no question of their existing independently of matter. Yet unlike a person's essence, the soul's essence does not comprise both matter and form as constituent parts but is form alone. Any soul, the souls of brutes included, has a simple and not a composite essence. Being form alone and not a composite of form and matter, no soul as soul includes matter as a constituent

---

[134] ——, *Summa contra gentiles*, trans. J.F. Anderson, Book II, chap. 69, 6, 208 (parentheses and italics are mine).

part of its definition. But if that is so, then it is no contradiction after all to say that the soul can exist without matter.

To this it might be countered that Aquinas avoids the contradiction in this way only by surrendering his belief that the soul depends on matter for its concept or essence. True, if matter does not in the first instance enter into the concept of the soul as one of its constituent parts, then Aquinas cannot be charged with a contradiction in terms in affirming that the soul does not depend on matter to exist. But the trouble is that to embrace the antecedent here seems to imply that the soul is independent of matter in concept as well as in existence.

To this counter-objection Aquinas would reply by distinguishing two ways in which the definition of one concept depends on another concept.[135] One can say that one concept depends on another either intrinsically or extrinsically. To say that the definition of a concept c intrinsically depends on another concept d is to say that d is a constituent part of the definition of c. Thus, the concept *stone* depends on body because the concept of body is the genus of stone. When a concept depends on another concept in this way, it is evidently a contradiction in terms to affirm that any instance of c exists or can exist independently of d. A stone is inconsistently said to be incorporeal. However, to say that the definition of a concept c extrinsically depends on another concept d is to say that one cannot define c without adverting to something (d) which, so far from its being a constituent part of c, is utterly opposed and alien to c. Thus, one cannot define the concept of the actuation of something without bringing in the opposed notion of potentiality. In a loose sense, one can say that potentiality "enters into" the definition of actuation. But it does not enter into it as one of its constituent parts. Otherwise the contradiction ensues that the actuation of what is potential is itself something potential. As it is with actuation and potentiality, so is it with the concepts of form and matter. You cannot define form without bringing in the notion of matter. Yet, matter is not a constituent part of form. Otherwise form would be matter.

Suppose, then, that it is conceded that a soul is a certain form, i.e. the substantial form of a body. Then the concept of body cannot enter into the concept of the soul as one of its constituent parts any

---

[135] ——, *On Being and Essence*, trans. A. Maurer, chap. 6, 55.

more than matter can in this way enter into the concept of any other form. Otherwise the soul would be body and not the form of a body. Even so, the concept of soul does in a sense conceptually depend on the concept of body just as any form conceptually depends on matter. To say this is to say that, taken in and of itself soul has an incomplete essence, the incompleteness being completed by the concept of body. But because its completion by body is a completion by something that is both opposed and logically posterior to it, it is not contradictory to say that the soul can exist without body. It is no more contradictory to say this than it is to say that form can exist without matter, actuality can exist without potentiality, or substance can exist without accident. And this is for the same reason. For here again, matter, potentiality, and accident are both opposed and logically posterior to form, actuality, and substance, respectively.

Quite generally, then, one can say that whenever one concept c extrinsically depends on another concept d such that d is both opposed to and logically posterior to c, then one consistently says that c can exist independently of d. So even though concepts like form, actuality, and soul conceptually depend on the opposite notions of matter, potentiality and body, respectively, there need not be existential dependence of the former on the latter. True, we cannot define form, actuality, and soul without adverting to the concepts of matter, potentiality and body, respectively. Still, that this conceptual dependence is extrinsic and not intrinsic and that the latter are logically posterior to the former imply that one consistently says that form, actuality, and soul can exist independently of matter, potentiality and body, respectively.

In summary: that Aquinas's view of the soul is paradoxical no one can deny. But paradox is not contradiction. One compatibly says both that the soul is the form of the body and that it is independent of the body. It all depends on what in this context it is meant by 'independent.' For the reasons given, Aquinas denies that form necessarily depends on matter existentially just because it depends on matter essentially or for its definition.[136] Further, he affirms that it is possible that the soul's powers follow its being in the sense of its existence as well as its essence. That this possibility is in fact actualized is shown by the fact of human understanding. If the status of a power

---

[136] ——, *On Being and Essence*, tans. A. Maurer, chap. 4, 44.

is shown by its act and if actual understanding is independent of matter then so too is the power of understanding from which it springs. That same power, therefore, must follow on the soul's existence and not its essence. For since matter enters into the human essence, powers that flow from the latter are not independent of matter. Their subject is not the soul alone but the composite of soul and body. If, then, i) power follows being, ii) the power of understanding is independent of matter and material conditions, and iii) a person's being in the sense of essence includes matter, then the paradox in question follows. While the soul's being in the sense of essence depends on matter in the sense specified, the soul's being in the sense of its existence is nonetheless subsistent or independent of matter.

Chapter Nine
Dialectical Mind

In Chapter Five it was asked what must be added to true belief to get knowledge. However, thought is wider than either believing or knowing. One can think about something without either having belief or knowledge about it. Jones might wonder if Smith is at home without either believing or knowing that he is at home and wondering is a form of thinking. Or one might propose or consider an idea without either believing or disbelieving it, and considering and proposing ideas or propositions are forms of thinking. Scholastic philosophers distinguish simple apprehension, judgment and reasoning as forms of thought or thinking. The last includes but goes beyond the first two. Syllogisms include three judgments and the latter, as they occur in the syllogism, include three concepts that are known by simple apprehension. The syllogism is a process of mediation in which two of the three concepts are linked in the conclusion by virtue of their being linked to the third in the premises. To the extent that the syllogism employs mediation by means of which knowledge in the conclusion includes but yet goes beyond that of the premises, syllogistic reasoning can be called dialectical thinking.

In any case, this final chapter focuses on this type of thinking or thought. By some of its proponents such as Hegel it is knowledge considered in its progress or development, so that to speak of dialectical thinking is to speak of degrees of knowing and degrees of truth. This progress or development of knowledge is characterized by the movement of finite minds, and in the case of absolute Idealists like Hegel the Infinite Mind, from one idea to its opposite and from there to a more concrete, complete and hence truer and more real synthesis of the two. The first phase in this triad represents a one-sided unity, the second a one-sidedness on the opposite side of plurality, and the third the inclusion and elevation of these first two phases onto a higher plain. And for Hegel this dialectical progression of knowledge characterized objective thought or reality and not just human subjective thinking.

Hegel, like Aquinas, owed much to Aristotle. St. Thomas' indebtedness goes without saying. As for Hegel, J. N. Findlay warns of the danger of ignoring the extent to which Hegel's philosophy is Hellenic.[137] William Wallace states that Hegel's philosophy "...is conscious of its continuity and proud of its identity with the teachings of Plato and Aristotle..."[138] W.T. Stace observes that the underlying substance of the philosophies of Plato, Aristotle and Hegel comprise one universal philosophy, despite their individual differences.[139] As regards method in particular, Hans-Georg Gadamer contends that though it differs from the dialectic of ancient philosophers, Hegel's dialectic has its roots in ancient dialectic. It goes back to ancient dialectic in a more explicit way "than would have ever entered the minds of anyone before Hegel, either in the Middle Ages or the modern period."[140] According to Gadamer, Hegel "...worked out his own dialectical method by extending the dialectic of the Ancients and transforming it into a sublimation of contradiction into ever higher syntheses."[141] And G.R.G. Mure, who thinks that the best introduction to Hegel is the study of Aristotle, points out that Hegel himself attests to his Aristotelian roots.[142] Mure alludes approvingly to Hegel's statement that Aristotle's *De Anima* is "the best work on the philosophy of spirit and that the chief goal of such a philosophy is to reinterpret the teaching of that work".[143] Given the centrality of dialectic in Hegel's philosophy, this suggests that Hegel construes Aristotle's philosophy and in particular his philosophy of mind as a form of dialectic thought. But if so, and if Hegel is right that Aristotle employs dialectic thought in that form, then one should expect to find that form of dialectic at work in the thought of Aquinas as well. It is the aim of this chapter to show that such is in fact the case, even though

---

[137] J. N. Findlay, *Hegel: A Re-examination* (London: Allen and Unwin, 1958), 22. See also, 48, 216.

[138] William A. Wallace, trans. *Hegel's Philosophy of Mind* (London: Oxford University Press, 1894), xiii-xiv.

[139] W.T. Stace, *The Philosophy of Hegel* (New York: Dover Publications, 1955), 4.

[140] Hans-Georg Gadamer, *Hegel's Dialectic: Five Hermeneutical Studies*, trans. by P. Christopher Smith (New Haven: Yale University Press, 1976), 12.

[141] *Ibid.*, 31.

[142] G.R. G. Mure, *An Introduction to Hegel* (London: Oxford University Press, 1959) Preface, xii.

[143] *Ibid.*, Preface, xii.

the Hegelian dialectic cannot simply be read back into the philosophies of either Aquinas or Aristotle.

I. Dialectic and Some Philosophers

To begin, Hegel himself insists that the dialectic method is not unique to him. He mentions Plato who used it in its objective form.[144] He singles out the *Parmenides* as being perhaps "the greatest literary product of ancient dialectic...".[145] As to this influence of the *Parmenides* on Hegel, Gadamer states that Hegel construes Plato's dialectic in that dialogue as positive, i.e. as producing contradictions like being and non-being not merely "to nullify their presuppositions" but "to entail a higher unity".[146] Further, Charles Taylor points out the similarity of what he calls Hegel's ontological dialectic to Plato's pointing to contradictions in formulae that are proffered as definitions of a given idea or standard, thus causing those formulae to be abandoned for more adequate ones.[147] Moreover, Hegel himself says that Socrates used dialectic in its subjective shape in Socratic irony. Socrates, says Hegel, used dialectic first against ordinary consciousness and then against the Sophists.[148] By contrast, some ancient philosophers never got further than the understanding, the source of abstractions and hard and fast distinctions, and with that went no further than the mere universality of Ideas.[149] Thus is dialectic frozen or put on

---

[144] Hegel, *The Encyclopaedia of the Philosophical Sciences* in W. Wallace, trans., *The Logic of Hegel* (London: Oxford University Press, 1959) no. 81, 149

[145] Hegel, *Phenomenology of Mind*, translated by J.B. Baillie, in J. Loewenberg, ed., *Hegel Selections* (New York:, 1929), 65.

[146] Hans-Georg Gadamer, *Hegel's Dialectic: Five Hermeneutical Studies*, trans. by P. Christopher Smith (New Haven: Yale University Press, 1976), 21. Gadamer goes on to state (p. 22) that Hegel thinks that dialectic in the *Sophist* has the same sense that it has in the *Parmenides*, but that in this Hegel is mistaken.

[147] Charles Taylor, *Hegel* (Cambridge: Cambridge University Press, 1975), 133. Taylor refers particularly to *Republic* I when Cephalus defines justice as telling the truth and giving back what one owes.

[148] Hegel, *The Encyclopaedia of the Philosophical Sciences*, in W. Wallace, trans. *The Logic of Hegel*, no. 81, 149.

[149] This drawing of hard and fast distinctions in philosophy Hegel characterizes as dogmatism. See Hegel, *The Encyclopaedia of the Philosophical Sciences*, in W. Wallace, trans., *The Logic of Hegel*, no. 32, 66–67.

hold. Here, he singles out the Eleatics who fixated on Being, and Heraclitus who fixated on Becoming. To that extent both philosophies can be charged with formalism.[150] True, becoming is the synthesis of and hence more concrete than either being or non-being. But even becoming needs to advance dialectically in depth and meaning and does so in the higher concept of life and especially of mind.[151] Hegel cites the philosophies of Parmenides and Heraclitus as examples of the refutation of one system by another. For the refutation of a philosophy, says he, consists in showing "the dialectical movement in its principle", thus reducing it "to a constituent member of a higher concrete form of the Idea".[152] Hegel goes on to say that the dialectic appears most notably in Kant's list of categories where the third category in each group of three is the synthesis of the first two as well. It is even more significantly found in Kant's antinomies.[153] The latter show that "every abstract proposition of understanding, taken precisely as it is given, veers round into its opposite".[154] This is dialectic in the sense of the assertion of two opposite predicates of one and the same subject. Thus the thesis of the first antinomy affirms that the world had a beginning in time and is limited as regards space while its antithesis denies that the world had beginning in time and is spatially limited. Hegel states that the importance of Kant's antinomies is that their existence hastened the downfall of the rigid dogmatism of the metaphysics of understanding, thus directing attention to dialectic thought. Though unrecognized by Kant himself, the real meaning of his antinomies was to show that "every actual thing involves a coexistence of opposed elements"[155] These Platonic and Kantian senses of 'dialectic' are related to but not Hegel's sense of the term. He says that in its true and proper character dialectic is "the very nature and essence of everything predicated by mere understanding — the law of things and of the finite as a whole."[156] It is "the indwelling tendency outwards by which the one-sidedness and limitation of the predicates of understanding is seen in its true light,

---

[150] *Ibid.*, no. 12, 21.
[151] *Ibid.*, no. 88, 168.
[152] *Ibid.*, no. 88, 168.
[153] *Ibid.*, no. 81, 149.
[154] *Ibid.*, no. 81, 149.
[155] *Ibid.*, no. 48, 99–100.
[156] *Ibid.*, no. 81, 149.

and shown to be the negation of them."¹⁵⁷ Here the emphasis is on negativity. When properly seen, the predicates of understanding are not viewed as static and isolated but as dynamic, as canceling themselves out and passing into their opposites not by anything external but by their very own acts or natures.

Conspicuous by its absence in this context is reference by Hegel to Schelling and especially to Fichte. As has often been pointed out, the terms, 'thesis', 'antithesis' and 'synthesis' by which the triadic movement of the dialectic is so often named, appear much more frequently in Fichte's works than in Hegel's. Nor can it be plausibly argued that they have a non-dialectic use in the former. Also, no reference is made here to the presence of dialectic in Aristotle's philosophy. Yet as Mure shows, the influence of Aristotle on Hegel's philosophy overall and on his idea of dialectic development in particular cannot be denied.¹⁵⁸ Hegel's philosophy is in Mure's view "a direct development of the Aristotelian philosophy".¹⁵⁹

To spell this out, dialectic characterizes Aristotle's analysis of change in the *Physics*. The latter foreshadows Hegel's view that dialectic can be seen in the fact that sensible things are changeable. Both philosophers construe this as implying that such things are and yet are not, thus illustrating the contradictory or seeming contradictory character of dialectic. This is explicitly stated by Hegel.¹⁶⁰ And it comes out in Aristotle's answer to the Parmenidean dilemma of change. That dilemma can be seen as a classic case of a philosopher's being misled by and getting stuck on either horn due to the false abstraction of the understanding (*verstand*). For the latter, the concepts being and non-being are hard and fast, excluding each other and exhibiting no common ground. They are strangers to each other. Hence the dilemma of becoming which for the abstractive understanding is ineluctable. If being comes to be then it must come to be either from being or from non-being, and neither is possible. So all becoming is illusory. Hegel thinks that this *a priori* ruling out of change or becoming is just what happens when the understanding does its work of abstraction, cutting off and isolating concepts from each other. In any case, Aristotle's answer can be construed dialectically. For it in-

---

[157] Ibid.,, no. 81, 149.
[158] G. R. G. Mure, *An Introduction to Hegel*, 52-53.
[159] Ibid., 58.
[160] Hegel, *The Encyclopaedia of the Philosophical Sciences*, no. 32, 67.

volves saying that being in a sense comes out of non-being in which it is hidden. The meaning of 'in a sense' is important here, and spelling it out shows the difference between Aristotle's and Hegel's dialectic. To take a concrete case, if when Socrates becomes musical, musical is said to come to be either from musical itself as abstracted or cut off from anything else or from non-musical taken in the same way, then Parmenides is right. It is impossible for Socrates to become musical. For the musical as such cannot become the non-musical as such, nor *vice versa*. There is a strict "either-or" between them, the one excluding the other and neither one of them being a condition of the other. If you go by the abstractive understanding, or as Hegel sometimes says, if you go by the rigid formality of concepts, then logic *a priori* rules out becoming.

Aristotle's answer to the dilemma is that while musical as such cannot come to be from non-musical as such (or *vice versa*), yet musical can come to be from non-musical just because that from which musical does come to be (i.e. the complex of non-musical Socrates) implicitly includes musical. In that sense, says Aristotle, it can be said that being comes out of non-being. It comes out of non-being not as such but incidentally. That implies that the two are united in a larger whole. Being is said to come out of non-being in the sense that the whole out of which being comes, i.e. non-musical Socrates, is not without non-being. For it harbors the privation of musical. In terms of the example, so far from there being a strict 'either-or' as between the musical and the non-musical, the contrary of this rigidity of dogmatism (as Hegel calls it) prevails.[161] The musical and the non-musical are in different ways united in the larger whole, Socrates. There is an identity of opposites. Another way of putting it is that musical does not come to be either from non-musical simply or from musical in act but from musical in potency. And musical in potency gets between both non-musical simply and musical in act. Because things that actually come to be preexist potentially with their opposites in a certain concrete whole, it can be said both that being comes to be from being without saying either that being in act comes to be from being in act and that being comes to be from non-being without saying that being comes to be from non-being as such.

---

[161] *Ibid.*, no. 32, 66–67.

Though this comes closer to Hegel's dialectic than do the Platonic or Kantian dialectics, it is not Hegel's dialectic. Aristotle does not hold and for him it is impossible that *concepts* harbor their opposites and go over to the latter, so that, for example, the concept being includes the concept non-being which comes out of it. This kind of identity of opposites he would reject as being a conceptual contradiction paralleling the propositional contradiction "P is true and P is not true". He says instead that a *thing* that changes, say water that becomes warm, is an identity of opposites in the sense that one and the same water is at once actually cool and potentially warm, and that is a different matter. Even so, one can see the shadow of the foregoing Aristotelian assay of change in Hegel's remark to the effect that there is no 'either-or' anywhere in the world but instead everything tends to its opposite. Thus,

> .... Neither in heaven nor in earth neither in the world of mind nor of nature, is there anywhere such an abstract 'Either-or' as the understanding maintains. Whatever exists is concrete, with difference and opposition in itself. The finitude of things will then lie in the want of correspondence between their immediate being and what they essentially are. Thus, in inorganic nature, the acid is implicitly at the same time the base: in other words, its only being consists in its relation to its other. Hence also the acid is not something that persists quietly in the contrast: it is always in effort to realize what it potentially is.... [162]

Moreover, this effort in something to realize its potential shows another element in Hegel's dialectic that is traced to Aristotle. That is the idea of inner design or immanent teleology. Acid or for that matter anything else is always in an effort to realize what it potentially is just because the latter resides in it as end or goal. This inner design moves the dialectic process like an Aristotelian immanent final cause.[163] Referring approvingly to Aristotle as regards this idea of inner teleology, Hegel says,

---

[162] *Ibid.*, no.119, 223.
[163] It goes without saying that Hegel rejects any form of transcendent final cause i.e. a final cause that is above and beyond the world such as some end or goal for the world or worldly event in the mind of a God that is external to the world.

By End, however we must not at once, nor must we ever merely, think of the form which it has in consciousness as a mode of mere mental representation. By means of the notion of inner design Kant has resuscitated the Idea in general and particularly the idea of life. Aristotle's definition of life virtually implies inner design, and is thus far in advance of the notion of design in modern Teleology, which had in view finite and outward design only.[164]

By saying that Aristotle's definition of life implies inner design, Hegel apparently refers to Aristotle's view that though individual organisms cannot achieve eternality by uninterrupted continuity (since they perish), yet they try to achieve that end by continuing their existence in things *like* themselves, i.e. by continuing their uninterrupted oneness not as individuals but as species.[165] And this unconscious purpose in living things shows that Aristotle recognizes inner design, according to Hegel. In any case and in general, the antithesis lay hidden in the thesis as the latter's goal, and in its turn the antithesis harbors the synthesis as *its* end or goal. Ultimately the goal of the whole dialectic process is the Idea in and for itself (Spirit) in which the preceding stages of the idea in itself (Logic) and the Idea for itself (Nature) are included but raised to a higher form. Hegel compares this ultimate goal of Spirit or the Idea in and for itself with Aristotle's God (which for him is the final end of all movement) thinking itself. (νοησις νοησεως). Thus,

...The defect of life lies in its being only the idea implicit or natural: whereas cognition is in an equally one-sided way the merely conscious idea, or idea for itself. The unity and truth of these two is the absolute idea, which is both in itself and for itself. Hitherto we have had the idea in development through its various grades as our object, but now the idea comes to be its own object. This is the νοησις νοησεως which Aristotle long ago termed the supreme form of the idea.[166]

---

[164] Hegel, *The Encyclopaedia of the Philosophical Sciences*, no. 204, 345.
[165] Aristotle, *On the Soul* in R. McKeon, ed., *The Basic Works of Aristotle* (New York: Random House, 1941) Bk. II, Ch. 4, 415b, 4-7, 561.
[166] Hegel, *The Encyclopedia of the Philosophical Sciences*, no. 236, 374.

II. Hegelian Dialectic in the Triad of Notion, Judgment
and Syllogism

A case of this immanent teleology in which the end has a higher degree of knowledge and reality than what strives toward it is the relation of notion to judgment. Hegel contrasts the merely external view of judgment found in formal logic with this richer account. The former construes judgment as a combination of subject and predicate in which the subject is outside our heads and the predicate inside. Thus, subject and predicate are merely external to each other. This account is also merely external in that subject and predicate are viewed as contingent. By this he means that this assay fails to see that the judgment is the particularization of the notion. Judgment shows the specific character of the subject being imposed on it by the self-differentiating notion. So judgment is the self-unraveling by the notion of what is already implicit in the notion. Hegel uses the following analogy:

> Thus, for example, as we remarked before, the germ of the plant contains its particular, such as root, branches, leaves, etc: but these details are at first present only potentially, and are not realized till the germ uncloses. This unclosing is, as it were, the judgment of the plant....[167]

As the germ or seed already contains roots, branches and leaves, so too the notion already contains the judgment. In each case the latter is in the former as plan or end. As roots, branches and leaves are the particularization of the seed, so too are various predicates so many particularizations of the subject or notion. Every judgment is of the form 'the individual is the universal'. These are the terms, says Hegel, under which subject and predicate confront each other. Yet the copula expresses not just difference but identity too. The notion or subject goes out of itself and over to its opposite, the universal or predicate, thus specifying or particularizing itself. Yet while all the while differentiating itself in various predicates, the notion identifies itself with those predicates. The individual is said *to be* the universal. What ultimately drives the notion to actively specify itself in this

---

[167] *Ibid.*, no. 166, 299.

way is none other than the Absolute, functioning as internal final cause within the notion, aiming at its own self-manifestation.

Still, the dialectic process does not end here. For as the judgment lay hidden in the notion, so does the syllogism lay hidden in the judgment. And Hegel suggests that the syllogism is the unity or synthesis of notion and judgment. It includes both but raises them to a higher level. Thus,

> The syllogism brings the notion and the judgment into one. It is notion,—being the simple identity into which the distinctions of form in the judgment have retired. It is judgment, — because it is at the same time set in reality, that is, put in the distinction of its terms...[168]

The movement from judgment to syllogism is not made just by us i.e. subjectively. It is also objective. As W.T. Stace puts it, the syllogism for Hegel "is not to be regarded as a merely subjective form of thought. Like the judgment, it is objective. Everything is a syllogism. Or, more correctly, because the syllogism is the form of *reason*, therefore everything *rational*, i.e. everything *actual*, is a syllogism."[169] Syllogistic reasoning is the judgment itself which "puts itself as syllogism, and in the conclusion returns to the unity of the notion."[170] Hegel thinks that objectively speaking the syllogism lay hidden in the judgment as well as in the notion. It does so, says he, by the particular becoming "the mediating mean between the individual and the universal."[171] In a qualitative syllogism, the general syllogistic schema S=M=P becomes I=P=U where a subject as individual comes to be linked to a universal by means of a particularizing quality.[172] What Hegel means is that in, say, "All whales are mammals and Willie is a whale, so Willie is a mammal", the particularization of Willie in the minor premise is 'whale'. But 'whale' (call it P for particular) is also what mediates the individual Willie (I) and the universal mammal (U). The particular P is the subject of the universal but the predicate of the individual. So here one can say that the individual Willie (I) by

---

[168] *Ibid.*, no. 181, 314
[169] W.T. Stace, *The Philosophy of Hegel*, 248.
[170] Hegel, *The Encyclopedia of the Philosophical Sciences*, no. 181, 315.
[171] *Ibid.*, no. 181, 314
[171] *Ibid.*, no. 181, 315.
[172] *Ibid.*, no. 183, 317.

means of its particularization 'whale' (P) "connects itself with U, its universal or notion"[173] The syllogism can thus be construed as the process whereby by mediation individuals like Willie go out of themselves to their particularizations (in this case, "Willie is a whale), in order to come back to themselves as universals in the conclusion (in this case, "Willie is a mammal"). In this process, the individual taken as such is the thesis, the particularization it goes over to is the antithesis (which in any Hegelian triad signifies mediation) and the universal it comes back to in the conclusion is the synthesis, representing as it does the identity or union of opposites, i.e. I and U. The union of individual and universal in the conclusion represents the return of the thesis (the individual taken as such) to itself on a higher level of rationality (since U is higher than P) and hence reality. In this triad the subject term Willie represents the individual in and of itself (thesis), the judgment "Willie is a whale' represents the individual for itself or going out of itself (antithesis), and the conclusion represents the individual in and for itself (synthesis) which includes the two though elevated to a higher level. The conclusion represents the idea or thesis Willie as having returned to itself by dint of its having gone out of itself in its self-particularization in the minor premise "Willie is a whale". Hegel says that a syllogism of this sort has in it "an immediately individual thing as subject", in this case 'Willie'. This is the thesis which as always has the character of immediacy. Then a particular aspect of this subject is selected, in this case 'whale'. This is the antithesis which as always has the character of mediation. Finally and by means of the latter the individual "turns out to be a universal", as in this case and in the conclusion Willie comes back to itself as, or turns out to be, mammal.[174] This is the synthesis which includes but overcomes the one-sidedness of the bare immediacy or unity of the thesis and the bare mediation, particularity or difference of the antithesis. Since he sees this linking of individual and universal by a mediating particular as the essence of the syllogism and since he holds that everything that exists is a particular which joins together the individual and the universal, Hegel says that "the syllogistic form is a universal form of all things."[175]

---

[173] *Ibid.*, no. 181, 315.
[174] *Ibid.*, no. 183, 317.
[175] *Ibid.*, no. 24, 50.

A final point in his connection is that whereas simple apprehension and judgment represent for Hegel the thesis and antithesis stages, respectively, of any triad, the syllogism for him represents the synthesis stage.[176] The thesis is the stage of simple apprehension or one-sided unity or identity, the antithesis is the stage of judgment or one-sided difference, and the synthesis is the stage of the syllogism, i.e. a unity-in-difference. For in syllogisms major and minor terms are united by the common ground of middle terms. For example, in the triad: being, nothing, becoming, the thesis being is first simply apprehended without any judgment being made about it. But when in the antithesis being goes out of itself and moves to its opposite (i.e. nothing), judgment then comes into play. That is because in the passage from being to nothing simple self-identity and immediacy goes over to difference and mediation. No longer is being just being as in the thesis but being (A) is in this antithesis said to be its other (B) i.e. nothing, and this implies the judgment, "Being is nothing" or "A is B". Thus, as the thesis is identity and the antithesis difference, so the thesis represents simple or unitary apprehension and the antithesis represents the diversity (i.e. "A is B") of judgment. Finally, the third term or synthesis, i.e. becoming, is identity-in-difference. It includes both being and nothing as both distinguished and yet united on a higher level. In so doing it represents the syllogism. For "P is U, I is P, and therefore I is U" expresses the unity-in-difference of individual (I) and universal (U) on a higher level in the conclusion by dint of I's being the subject of P in the second premise and U's being the predicate of P in the first premise.

III. Dialectic in Aquinas' Triad of Sensation, Apprehension and Judgment

To move to Aquinas, one must state straight off that nothing in his thought corresponds to the Hegelian idea of the Absolute's dialectic self-unfolding in order to reach a state of final self-consciousness. Aquinas' God is neither identified with the whole of reality nor does it go through a dialectic process of unfolding itself in finite manifestations of itself in order to attain perfect self-knowledge. For one

---

[176] See W.T. Stace, *The Philosophy of Hegel*, 125-126.

thing Aquinas' God is not in progress and hence not striving toward self-consciousness or any other end. For another, so far from being identified with Hegel's Absolute, the Judaic-Christian God represents what Hegel calls the wrong idea of the infinite, i.e. a God that transcends and is separate from the world.[177]

Even so, besides his account of change in general which exactly follows Aristotle's dialectic assay of the same, Aquinas' philosophy of mind exemplifies dialectic movement on two fronts. There is the cognitive change in knowers from sensation to simple apprehension and from the latter to judgment.[178] Second there is the movement from premises to conclusions in syllogisms. As to the first, Aquinas holds that since it belongs to the nature of a body to exist in some particular body or other, then no body can ever be adequately known except insofar as it exists in this or that individual body.[179] However, since we know what is individual only through the senses (and secondarily through the imagination) it follows that in order to know its proper object, i.e. corporeal natures, our minds must turn to phantasms (sense images) in order to perceive corporeal natures adequately, i.e. *as existing*.[180]

That said, it is the mental act by which this turning to phantasms occurs that exemplifies dialectic. And in the view of Aquinas that act is judgment. It is by the subject-predicate judgment that our intellects refer the abstract universals of simple apprehension back to the concrete particulars of sense from which they were first abstracted.[181] Thus,

> ...Hence our intellect knows directly only universals. But indirectly, however, and by a kind of reflexion, it can know the singular, because, as we have said above, even after abstracting the intelligible species, the intellect, in order to

---

[177] *Ibid.*, no. 45, 93.

[178] As stated previously, dialectic logic in both Aristotle and Aquinas is similar to but not the same as Hegel's dialectic. Hegel took up the Aristotelian dialectic but altered it for his own purposes.

[179] St. Thomas Aquinas, *The Summa Theologica* , translated by Fathers of the English Dominican Province, (Chicago: Encyclopaedia Britannica, 1952) vol. I, I, Q. 84, Art. 7, 449-450.

[180] *Ibid.*, vol. I, I, Q. 84, Art. 7, 449-450.

[181] By 'first' here it is not necessarily meant temporally first. But what is meant is logically first.

understand actually, needs to turn to the phantasms in which it understands the species, as said in *De Anima* iii. Therefore, it understands the universal directly through the intelligible species, and indirectly the singular represented by the phantasm. *And thus it forms the proposition, "Socrates is a man."* [182]

To bring this out, suppose that on a trip to the Andes S becomes acquainted with birds which she later learns are condors. Through this experience S forms a general idea of the bird. Suppose too that subsequently S focuses on a particular bird she calls Cletus and truly judges that Cletus is a condor. Here, unlike the simple apprehension by which S initially grasps the nature of a condor in the abstract, S applies that general notion to Cletus with whom she is presently acquainted. Whereas the simple apprehension of the universal condor is an act of analysis whereby S extracts the species from several instances of it (i.e. total abstraction) and understands that species as abstracted and isolated from the real existence it has in things, the judgment, "Cletus is a condor" is by contrast an act of synthesis whereby S mentally reunites that same species to the individual Cletus. Thus, it is by means of the subject–predicate judgment that S overcomes the abstraction of simple apprehension. And she does this by referring abstract predicates to the concrete particulars signified by the corresponding subjects of those predicates, the latter being presented to us in sense or imagination. By so doing, S understands the natures of things (in this case the nature of being a condor) not as such but as existing. For if as Aquinas states, it belongs to the nature of a condor or any other material thing to exist in some particular condor or other, and if that is exactly the way S understands a condor in her judgment, "Cletus is a condor", then it is only in and through a judgment of this sort that S really comes to understand what a condor is. But since judgments like this require that those who make them turn back to sense images as the subjects of these judgments, it follows that our minds must turn back to sense images in order to know corporeal natures adequately, i.e. as existing as opposed to as conceived. Thus does Aquinas hold with empiricists and as against extreme rationalists that knowledge of fact or existence is

---

[182] St. Thomas Aquinas, *Summa theologica*, vol. I, I, Q. 86, Art. 1, 461 (emphasis is mine).

gained not by abstract understanding alone but by the cooperation or union of understanding and sense, of simple apprehension coupled with the subject-predicate judgment.

That aside and to specify Aquinas' assay of the subject-predicate judgment, the latter consists, says he, in a relation of identity. What this means is shown by contrasting the orders of logic and reality. In the latter, Socrates is distinct from the whiteness that is present in him. We could never say that Socrates is the whiteness that is present in him since no whole is identified with one of its parts.[183] No substance is one with one of its properties. Yet we can and do say in a subject-predicate judgment that Socrates is white, and here there is no question of predicating a part of a whole as there would be if we were to say that Socrates is whiteness or that he is his whiteness. That shows the difference between the two orders. In particular it shows the difference between the real relation of a thing and one of its properties and the logical relation of a subject and predicate. Whereas there is evidently no identity between a thing and one of its properties, none the less there *is* an identity between subject and predicate.[184] Otherwise we should no more be able to say that Socrates is white than we can say that he is his whiteness.

Moreover, as to the nature of this relation of logical identity between subject and predicate, it is none other than an identity of reference. To say that Socrates is white is to say that the very same thing to which 'Socrates' refers, i.e. the person of Socrates, is also the referent of the predicate 'white'. True, subject and predicate differ in sense or meaning. Yet they are the same in reference. To say that Socrates is white is to say that Socrates is this white thing.

Under this account of subject-predicate judgments, the latter stand at the apex of a cognitive triad that begins with sense perception, moves to simple apprehension and finally ends in those same subject-predicate judgments. We are first acquainted in sense perception with certain conglomerate wholes which we know in a vague, inchoate way. Then upon intellectual analysis of its parts or

---

[183] St. Thomas Aquinas, *On Being and Essence*, trans. A. Maurer, Chapter II, 37-38. See also, *The Summa theologica* translated by Fathers of the English Dominican Province, vol. II, Q. 85, Art. 5, Reply Obj. 3, 457-458.

[184] St. Thomas Aquinas, *Summa theologica*, translated by Fathers of the English Dominican Province, vol. II, Q.85, Art. 5, Reply Obj. 3, 458.

elements we come to know that whole more exactly and precisely.[185] The tool of this analysis is abstraction which begins with the simple apprehension of that whole's essence or nature. Thus, suppose that I see an object moving toward me on a plain at some distance. At first I only know that it is a moving object but I cannot yet tell whether it is a living thing or a type of motor vehicle. As it draws closer, I might determine that it is an animal though it is still unclear what sort of animal it is. As it draws closer still, I finally recognize that it is a buffalo.[186]

Here it is evident that I come to better know the approaching object because I see it in more detail as it draws closer. But it is important to see how this takes place. It does so through a tripartite process of cognition which occurs at each stage of that growing knowledge. First there is the sense perception of a complex individual whole. Second there is the simultaneous abstraction of a part or parts of that whole through and by means of which the sensed whole is analyzed into its parts for the sake of more precise knowledge. Third and last is the mental synthesis of judgment by which those abstracted parts are referred back to the sensed whole from which they were taken. The first stage of sense perception is an undifferentiated and unanalyzed unity. This is succeeded and overcome by the second stage in which mind enters the picture for the first time. Here mind selects and abstracts from the complex object of sense various features of the latter, focusing on these features in and of themselves for the sake of analysis. Therefore, as opposed to being an undifferentiated unity, this second stage is a specified diversity. It closely corresponds to Hegel's idea of a notion particularizing itself in a judgment.[187] It is mind as analyzing or breaking up the undifferentiated unity of the first stage. This it does by abstracting parts from that perceived unity or whole and expressing those particular parts by universal abstract ideas. Thus do I abstract 'condor', 'black', 'having a six-foot wingspan', etc. from Cletus. Finally, this second stage

---

[185] This does not imply nor does it seem to be the case that the order here is temporal. The 'first' and 'second' here refers to what is logically first and logically second.

[186] A similar example of this is given by St. Thomas. See St. Thomas Aquinas, *Commentary on Aristotle's Physics*, translated by Blackwell, Spath and Thirlkel, (New Haven: Yale University Press, 1963), Lecture 1, no. 11., 9.

[187] See above, 8–9.

of analysis by abstraction is superseded by the third and advanced stage of judgment. Here the abstracted parts in the predicates of these judgments remain distinct from their subjects or wholes and yet by means of the copula are simultaneously re-identified with those same sensed, existential subjects or wholes. And this for the sake of a higher type of knowledge than what is gained in the second stage of simple apprehension. Instead of being knowledge of the properties of things taken in themselves and just as such, it is knowledge of those properties as existing in fact and reality. Thus is this third and final stage of judgment knowledge neither of a one-sided undifferentiated unity of sense nor of an opposed one-sided abstracted diversity of mind. It is a synthesis in which both the unanalyzed unity and the analyzed diversity are taken up and absorbed in a larger whole. This unity-in-difference of sense and mind, of mind as referred to sense, is the subject-predicate judgment.

Construing this Thomistic cognitive triad of sense perception, apprehension and judgment as undifferentiated unity, abstract difference and a unity-in-difference, respectively, suggests the Hegelian pattern of thesis, antithesis and synthesis. For one thing, the sequence is from the general to the specific, just as is the case in the Hegelian dialectic.[188] For even though both sense images and their objects are individual, the knowledge which the former gives of the latter is vague and unspecified. This might be called general knowledge even though the generality here is one of sense and not of intellect. Aristotle says the following about this generality of sense:

> Now what is to us plain and obvious at first is rather confused masses, the elements and principles of which become known to us later by analysis. Thus we might advance from generalities to particulars; for it is a whole that is best known to sense-perception, and a generality is a kind of whole, comprehending many things within it, like parts. A name, e.g. 'round' means vaguely a sort of whole: its definition analyses this into its particular senses. Similarly a child

---

[188] For Hegel the synthesis in any triad is always more concrete and hence more real than either its thesis or its antithesis.

begins by calling all men 'father', and all women 'mother', but later on distinguishes each of them.[189]

Moreover, it is evident from his *Commentary on Aristotle's Physics* that Aquinas agrees with Aristotle in this.[190] For another thing, the triadic sequence from sense perception to apprehension to judgment in both Aquinas and Aristotle goes from a thing to its opposite and from there to a synthesis of the two in which the latter signifies a more concrete and improved knowledge than that which is had in the first two stages. So this is not a case of reading Hegel back into Aquinas' thought. It is a case of the dialectic existing first in the thought of Aristotle and Aquinas in one form and subsequently (through the influence of the former) in the philosophy of Hegel in another form. For behind Hegel (and Aquinas) is the philosophy of Aristotle.

To spell this out, it is evident that Aristotle held that sensation and understanding apprehend two opposed sorts of objects, i.e. individuals and universals.[191] Second, since he held that knowledge begins in sensation, Aristotle's view was that all knowledge moves from the one to the other. Hence, this movement proceeds from one opposite to another. We go in knowledge from sensing an object to having abstractive understanding of it. This does not imply that the former is temporally prior to the latter but it does imply that it is logically prior to the latter. Third, Aristotle holds that these opposites are not unrelated but that the first contains the second which is brought out of the first by an act of mind. True, Aristotle denies Hegel's idea that one concept contains its opposite, as for example, Hegel holds that the idea being logically contains the idea of non-being. This he would have regarded as contradictory, and as contradictions cannot in his view exist, then they cannot spur movement or change. Even

[189] Aristotle, *Physics*, translated by R.P. Hardie and R.K. Gaye in R. McKeon, ed., *The Basic Works of Aristotle* (New York: Random House, 1941), 184a, 22-184b, 14., 218.

[190] St. Thomas Aquinas, *Commentary on Aristotle's Physics*, translated by Blackwell, Spath and Thirlkel, Lecture 1, no. 9-11, p. 8-9. See also Aquinas, *Summa theologica* translated by Fathers of the Dominican Province I, Q. 85, art. 3, 455-456.

[191] Aristotle, *De Anima*, translated by J.A. Smith, in R. McKeon, ed., *The Basic Works of Aristotle* (New York: Random House, 1941), Book II, Ch. 5, 417b, 22-23, 566.

so, both philosophers agree that the universal is no separated Platonic Form. Any such real externality or separateness of the universal is denied by both philosophers. Instead, the universal is found in the particular with the result that our universal ideas, though opposed to the sense images from which they are abstracted, nonetheless fail to be entirely cut off from those images. Just as in the real order the universal lives in the singular, so too in the logical order are concepts latent in sense images.

Finally, both the sensation of individuals and the abstractive understanding of the universals that belong to it are for Aristotle one-sided and incomplete knowledge. Sensation fails to give us scientific knowledge of the individual and he joins Plato in according to the latter a higher type of knowledge. To the extent that it is bereft of scientific knowledge, therefore, the sensation of individuals is incomplete and inferior knowledge. Yet the abstractive understanding of universals is for its part one-sided too. It is tilted on the opposite side and hence incomplete. What is real for Aristotle is what is individual. Hence even though they have a foundation in the real, the abstracted universals of understanding are not themselves real. To the extent that they signify various parts of the real taken as such and apart from the real, they comprise a one-sided abstract diversity as opposed to the one-sided unanalyzed unity of sensation. This opposed one-sidedness of both sensation and abstract understanding is resolved and overcome only in judgment, which, while it preserves the difference between individual wholes and their abstracted parts in the form of its subject and predicate terms respectively, none the less achieves that a unity-in-difference which characterizes real individuals. And this it does by referring abstracted predicates back to their subjects by means of the copula 'is', as for example in the judgment "Cletus is a condor."

Now that Aquinas followed Aristotle in all this is evident from his example of real flesh and the essence of flesh in his *Commentary on Aristotle's De Anima*. Thus,

> But the being of flesh, i.e. its essence, must be discerned by some other faculty. But the functioning of two distinct faculties takes place in two ways. In one way flesh and its essence can be discerned by powers in the soul which are completely distinct; the essence discerned by the intellect, the flesh by the senses; and this happens when we know the

individual in itself and the specific nature in itself. But in
another way the flesh and its essence may be discerned, not
by two distinct faculties, but by one faculty knowing in two
distinct ways – knowing in one way flesh, in another the essence of flesh; and this happens when the knowing soul correlates the universal and the individual....
It (the intellect) knows the specific nature or essence of an
object by going out directly to that object; but it knows the
individual thing indirectly or reflexively, by a return to the
phantasms from which it abstracted what is intelligible.
This Aristotle expresses by saying that the intellectual soul
either knows flesh sensitively and discerns the 'being of
flesh' with 'another' and 'separate' potency, – i.e. other than
sensitivity, in the sense that intellect is a power distinct
from the senses; or it knows flesh and the 'being of flesh' by
one and he same intellectual power functioning diversely;
in so far as it can 'bend back', so to say, 'upon itself'. As
'stretched out straight', and apprehending directly, it 'discerns the being' or essence of flesh; but by reflection it
knows the flesh itself.[192]

Here Aquinas interprets Aristotle as holding that real or individual flesh and the essence of flesh can be known either by two distinct cognitive faculties, i.e. sense and intellect respectively, or by one faculty, intellect, knowing in two distinct ways. As to the first, I know my individual flesh by sense and also simultaneously understand universal flesh by simple apprehension. These two ways of knowing are opposites. The object of one is individual while the object of the other is universal. Aquinas also indicates that each knowledge here is one-sided and incomplete. For what sense knows is individual flesh *in itself*, (i.e. as unrelated to the universal flesh) and what intellect understands through apprehension is the specific nature flesh *in itself*, (i.e. as unrelated to this or that individual flesh). As to the second, I know both individual flesh and the essence flesh simultaneously by one faculty i.e. intellect, knowing in two different ways. At one and the same time the intellect knows individual flesh one way and universal flesh another way. How does the intellect do this? Not by simple apprehension since it is only universal flesh in the abstract

---

[192] St. Thomas Aquinas, *Commentary on Aristotle's De Anima*, translated by K. Foster and S. Humphries (New Haven: Yale University Press, 1965) no. 712, 713, 416–417.

or flesh in itself that is known by that act. Aquinas' answer is that intellect simultaneously knows both individual flesh and universal flesh only when it "correlates the universal and the individual." This is what he describes both in the *Summa theologiae* and the *Commentary on Aristotle's De Anima* as the intellect's turning or returning to the phantasms.[193] Thus, while the intellect understands the universal directly and the sense knows the singular directly, nonetheless, says he, the intellect understands the singular indirectly by turning back to the phantasm after having abstracted the universal from the phantasm in simple apprehension. Thus, as is evident from the previous text from the *Summa theologiae*, Aquinas thinks that the act by which the intellect correlates the universal and the individual in this way — i.e. so as to understand the synthesis of the universal-in-the-particular — is the subject-predicate judgment.[194]

Granted that this movement from sensation to simple apprehension to judgment is dialectic in the sense explained, how can syllogistic reasoning be construed as a dialectical process? To answer, Aquinas' account of this third intellectual act also reveals dialectic movement just as it does for Hegel. Yet the dialectic is different in each case. For Hegel the syllogism is not just our subjective thinking, i.e. the syllogism of understanding. It is objective reason. True, it depends on mind but the mind here is objective Mind and not our minds.[195] It must be remembered that Hegel is an objective idealist. Since the real is the rational, that means that the syllogism with which he is concerned is real. At one point he says that everything is a syllogism.[196] That marks him off from both Aristotle and Aquinas for whom syllogisms are not real beings but beings of our reason which like concepts and judgments are human instruments of knowledge only.

Even so, whether the syllogism is taken as real being (Hegel) or as a human instrument by which real being is known (Aquinas), it is for both philosophers a dialectic process. It goes without saying that both philosophers agree on the basic law of the syllogism, i.e. *dici de*

---

[193] St. Thomas Aquinas, *Summa theologica*, translated by Fathers of the English Dominican Province, I, Q. 84, a. 7.

[194] See above, 12-13.

[195] Hegel, *The Encyclopaedia of Philosophical Sciences*, in W. Wallace, trans. *The Logic of Hegel*, no 181-182, 314-316.

[196] *Ibid.*, no. 181, 314.

omni ("to be said of all"). If P is found in every M and M is found in every S, then P is found in every S. Further, we saw that for Hegel the dialectic of the syllogism consists in the minor term S going out of itself in some particularization of itself (middle term) in the minor premise in order to return to itself on a higher level of universality (and hence of rationality) in the conclusion. Thus is the syllogism an advance in knowledge which for Hegel is *ipso facto* an advance in being.

IV. Aquinas' Dialectical Assay of the Syllogism

It remains to show in what sense Aquinas' view of the syllogism can be construed as a dialectic. Toward that end, though he has no direct treatment of the syllogism as such, Aquinas' thoughts on the syllogism in general can be gleaned from incidental remarks on the subject made in other contexts.[197] From these contexts it is clear that the heart of syllogistic reasoning for Aquinas (following Aristotle) is the idea of mediation through a middle term in the premises.[198] So the question is how and in what sense this mediate reasoning can be construed dialectically. What is the connection between mediation or mediated identity in the syllogism (i.e. S=M=P) and dialectic?

A plausible answer is that by its function of joining the S and P terms in the conclusion, the middle term is the means by which the one-sided wide generality of the P term in the major premise or rule and the opposite one-sided narrow particularity of the minor premise or case are both overcome in the conclusion which is the result of the rule and the case.[199] There the two are joined in a synthesis which

---

[197] See R.W. Schmidt, *The Domain of Logic According to Saint Thomas Aquinas* (The Hague: Martinus Nijhoff, 1966), 256–57.

[198] See Aristotle, *Posterior Analytics* in R. McKeon editor, *The Basic Works of Aristotle* (New York: Random House, 1941) Bk I, Chapter 19, 81b, 10–18, p. 136. See also Aquinas' Commentary on Book I of Aristotle's *Posterior Analytics*, 5, no 2; 9, no.4.

[199] C.S. Peirce labeled the propositions in deductive, inductive and abductive argument as either rule, case or result, their order being determined by the type of argument. See Charles Hartshorne and Paul Weiss, editors, *Collected Papers of Charles Sanders Peirce* (Cambridge: Harvard University Press, 1960), 2.619-2.631, 372–378. It is useful in explaining how the Aristotelian syllogism is a dialectic to follow Peirce in characterizing the major premise as a rule, the minor

gives new knowledge. Thus in the previous example, "All whales are mammals and Willie is a whale so Willie is a mammal", the one-sided wide generality of the P term in the major premise is overcome by its being linked in the conclusion to an opposite particular, i.e. the S term. By the same token, the one-sided narrow particularity of the S term in the minor premise is overcome by its being joined in the conclusion with an opposite generality, i.e. the P term. In a word, P's being linked to S tempers and corrects its relatively one-sided generality in the first premise. In so doing it preserves P and yet uplifts P in the sense that P figures in the new knowledge gained in the conclusion. By the same token, S's being linked to P in the same conclusion tempers and corrects its relatively one-sided particularity in the second premise. And once again this both preserves S and yet uplifts it due to S's participation in the new knowledge of the conclusion. The result (the conclusion) thus represents a unity or synthesis of universal and particular which constitutes a more advanced knowledge caused by the more direct or easier known premises. In this dialectic, the thesis can be said to be the one-sided generality of P in the major premise, the antithesis the one-sided individuality of S in the minor premise and the synthesis the union of both in the conclusion on a higher plain in the sense specified. Looked at from a somewhat different perspective, the rule (first premise) is the one-sided generality and may be regarded as the thesis. By contrast, the case which falls under the rule (second premise) is one-sided particularity and may be taken as the antithesis. Finally, the result of the rule and the case taken together (the conclusion) eliminates the respective one-sidedness of both rule and case by joining elements of both in a more balanced synthesis.

Yet though similar to Hegel's idea of syllogistic dialectic, this dialectical assay of the Aristotelian (and Thomistic) syllogism departs from Hegel's at least in three important respects. It was stated that the latter does not characterize reality itself but a logical instrument (the syllogism) through which we know reality. For St. Thomas, persons have their own agent or active intellects which not only perform the mental act of abstraction but which also move them from principles or premises to conclusions in syllogisms and other argu-

---

premise as a case of the rule and the conclusion as the result of both the rule and the case.

ments. In so doing they use the principles or premises as instruments as artisans use tools to make their products.[200] For him it is not any cosmic active intellect that does this, either in the form of a transcendent one like that of Averroes or an absolute immanent one like Hegel's. Hegel would agree with Aquinas so far as it concerns the human subjective syllogism. Each one of us has his or her own active intellect which makes syllogisms. But in addition to and behind these human or subjective syllogisms are what he calls objective syllogisms which characterize reality itself and which is the product of Absolute Mind or Spirit. Second, recall that for Hegel the S term goes out of itself in the minor premise in order to return to itself in the conclusion on a higher plain of universality or rationality. Here, the S term is the thesis and the M term is the antithesis. The conclusion (in this case 'Willie is a mammal') represents the synthesis of the abstract individual (in this case the S term 'Willie') and its equally abstract particularization (in this case the M-term 'whale'). The union of individual and universal in the conclusion represents this return of the thesis (the individual taken as such) to itself on a higher plain of universality (rationality) and hence of reality.

But it was stated that in the Aristotelian syllogistic none of the three concepts (S, M, or P) move to their opposites. It is individual substances as having the privation of an opposite form or property that go to those opposite forms or properties. Thus the concept non-musical does not become the concept musical (or *vice versa*) but it is non-musical Socrates who becomes musical Socrates. And in all of this Aquinas would agree. Finally, recall that for each philosopher the three stages in the syllogistic dialectic, i.e. what are commonly called the thesis, antithesis and synthesis, are different. For Hegel, the S term is the thesis, its particularization in the M term of the minor premise is the antithesis and the union of the S and P terms in the conclusion is the higher synthesis. But for both Aristotle and Aquinas, the thesis is the major premise as rule which when joined to the minor premise as case (antithesis) yields the new knowledge of the conclusion as result or synthesis.

---

[200] St. Thomas Aquinas, *Commentary on Aristotle's De Anima*, translated by K. Foster, S. Humphries and I. Thomas (New Haven: Yale University Press, 1965), Book III, chapter five, lecture ten, 429. See also, R.W. Schmidt, *The Domain of Logic According to St. Thomas Aquinas*, 254-255.

Nevertheless, it must be said that despite these differences, the dialectic of the syllogism is in one core respect the same for both philosophers. And that is that for each one the movement from premises to conclusion represents an advance both in knowledge and in intrinsic rationality. Recall that for Hegel the union of individual and universal in the conclusion represents the return of the thesis (the individual taken as such) to itself on a higher level of rationality and hence reality. In terms of our example, "All whales are mammals and Willie is a whale, so Willie is a mammal", the subject term 'Willie' represents the individual in and of itself, the judgment 'Willie is a whale' represents the individual for itself or going out of itself and the conclusion represents the individual in and for itself, which includes the first two though elevated to a higher level of intrinsic rationality.

By the same token, recall that for Aquinas and Aristotle both all reasoning (syllogistic or otherwise) proceeds from what is more evident to us in the premises to what is less evident to us in the conclusion.[201] It moves from what is directly evident to us to what, by dint of those premises, is indirectly evident to us.[202] Otherwise the latter or conclusion needs no proof. Moreover, even though it is less intelligible or evident *to us* than the premises, the conclusion is more intelligible or evident *in itself* than are the premises. That is because it adds specificity or concreteness to the general principle of the premise and form is the cause of specificity or concreteness. That means that the conclusion adds form to or actualizes the potentiality of the principle of the premise. For example, take the syllogism, "All wholes are greater than any one of their parts and organisms are wholes; so

---

[201] St. Thomas Aquinas, The *Summa theologica*, translated by Fathers of the English Dominican Province, Vol. II, Part I of the second Part, Q. 57, Art. 2, 36. See also *Summa theologica* I, Q.85, Art. 3; I, Q. 2, Art. 1; I, Q.14, Art. 7. See also Aristotle, *Physics,* Book I, chap. 1, 184a, 18–21.

[202] This more accurately describes the demonstrative than the dialectical syllogism. A condition of the former is that the premises are not just widely accepted (as in the case of dialectical syllogisms) but that they are both true and evident. Thus, valid demonstrative syllogisms give us certitude whereas valid dialectical syllogisms yield only reasonable opinion. (See Aristotle, *Topics* Book I, Chap. 1 (100a 25–31); *Posterior Analytics,* Book I, Chap. 6 (74b 5–25). See also Aquinas' *Commentary on Posterior Analytics* Book I, Chap. 6. Here, 'dialectical' is used in an entirely different sense than that in which it is being used throughout this paper.

all organisms are greater than any one of their parts." Here the conclusion adds specificity or concreteness to the general principle in the major premise. To do so it must add the form or difference "living" to the general idea of a whole. In so doing it actualizes the potentiality in the genus "whole". However, something is intelligible in itself to the extent that it is form or actuality as over against matter or potentiality. It follows that for Aquinas and Aristotle as for Hegel the new knowledge that is reached in conclusions of syllogisms expresses a higher level of intrinsic intelligibility or rationality than does the knowledge which is expressed in the premises. In other words, one moves from what is more easily known but intrinsically less intelligible or rational in the premises to what is less easily known and intrinsically more intelligible or rational in the conclusion. Moreover, this is quite consistent with saying that the principle of the premise is self-evident by nature as well as being self-evident to us, as for instance the first premise in the foregoing syllogism is self-evident by nature as well as being self-evident to us. For as is shown in this case, such general propositions are capable of being specified in the conclusion by the addition of a *differentia* or form and intrinsic intelligibility or rationality follows upon form.[203] Thus in different ways do Aquinas and Aristotle on one side and Hegel on the other share the same belief that syllogistic reasoning constitutes an advance in the intrinsic rationality of knowledge, the outstanding difference being that for Aristotle and Aquinas this increased rationality in knowledge is subjective, occurring in individual finite minds whereas for Hegel it is objective, charactering Reality or the Absolute Itself.

V. Summary

Hegel held that ancient Greek philosophy exemplified a form or stage of dialectic thought. In the case of the Eleatics, the dialectic reached the stage of understanding but advanced no further. The *a*

---

[203] For Aquinas, the proposition which has highest intrinsic intelligibility or rationality in this sense is the proposition "God exists". The latter is not just self-evident by nature (though not to us) since God is His own existence, but it also has highest intrinsic intelligibility or rationality because it expresses what is pure act or form without mix of potentiality. Perhaps the Hegelian analogue would be, "The Absolute is perfectly self-conscious".

priori argument of Parmenides to the effect that reality is one and changeless was based on the hard and fast opposition between the concepts of being and non-being and between the concepts of change and identity. These irreconcilable oppositions and the Parmenidean arguments to which they gave rise were the result of an incomplete dialectic, i.e. one in which mind, having become reduced to the level of understanding, advanced no further.

Further, dialectical mind showed itself in Plato's thought in the resolution of dilemmas raised by this same faculty of understanding. For example, in the *Meno* Plato overcomes the dilemma of knowing virtue by steering between the strict "either-or" outlook of understanding. Going by the latter, one is forced to say either that one knows what virtue is or that one does not. Either way excludes inquiry into virtue. The only way out is to outflank the rigid dichotomy of understanding, insisting (as does Plato) that this "either-or" stance of understanding is one-sided. In a sense one both knows and does not know what virtue is, says Plato. But to the extent that one says this, one's dialectic has passed beyond the stage of understanding.

Aristotle's thought exemplifies dialectic in that the founder of logic was also able to get beyond the stage of irreconcilable concepts. Instead of the "either-or" straightjacket of Eleatic thought, Aristotle used dialectical logic in his accounts of body and soul and becoming, to cite just two examples. And in this Aquinas followed Aristotle. Both philosophers deny that 'body' and 'soul' are totally opposed concepts as they are, for example, for Cartesian dualists. Instead, the one includes the other by reference. An organism's body is by definition one that is be-souled and the soul - even of a person - is by definition the form of a body. Neither concept is self-enclosed but to understand the one you must refer to the other. Moreover, changing things in some way contain their opposites. True, Socrates' being non-musical is a condition of his becoming musical, and understanding tells us that the two concepts are opposed. Yet the other side of the picture is that non-musical Socrates is also at the same time and in some way musical. Otherwise the change could never occur. Here, there is a half-truth in what Hegel says. Socrates must in some way already be musical in order to go from being non-musical to being musical. But that does not imply (nor did Aristotle and Aquinas think it did) that the *concept* 'non-musical' contains the opposite concept 'musical'.

Moreover, Hegel thinks that dialectical mind reached an even more advanced stage in Kant. Kant's tri-partite division of categories under quantity, quality, relation and modality moves beyond two starkly opposed categories to reach a third which in each group mediates the oppositions, thus forming a synthesis of the two. Thus under quantity, the category of totality can be construed as a synthesis of the opposed categories of unity and plurality. Moreover, Kant achieved a resolution of what he called the antinomies of pure reason by transforming the categories and forms of intuition from a state of being cut off from mind to being the creative manifestations of mind or the transcendental ego. For Hegel, by locating all categories in mind, Kant here took a first step toward overcoming irreconcilable oppositions in philosophy – oppositions that were caused by seeking truth by the understanding alone and relegating categories to things-in-themselves taken apart from Mind.

In any case, Hegel's dialectic can be seen at work in his treatment of the notion, the judgment and the syllogism. This parallels Aquinas' dialectic account of the triad of sensation, simple apprehension and judgment. Finally, for both Hegel and Aquinas the syllogism is construed dialectically, though the syllogistic dialectic takes a different form for each philosopher. In the case of Hegel, the general syllogistic schema S=M=P becomes in the qualitative syllogism I=P=U, where a subject as individual comes to be linked to a universal by means of a particularizing quality P. P is what mediates the individual (I) and the universal (U). The particular P is the subject of the universal but the predicate of the individual. So here one can say that the individual (I) by means of its particularization (P) links itself to U, its universal. The syllogism can thus be seen as the process whereby by mediation individuals go out of themselves to their particularizations in order to come back to themselves as universals in the conclusion. In this process, the individual taken as such is the thesis, the particularization it goes over to is the antithesis and the universal it comes back to in the conclusion is the synthesis, representing as it does the identity or union of opposites, i.e. I and U. The union of individual and universal in the conclusion signifies the return of the individual (I) to itself on a higher level of rationality (since U is higher than P) and hence reality. In this triad the subject term (I) represents the individual in and of itself (thesis), the minor premise represents the individual (I) for itself or I's going out of itself to P (antithesis), and the conclusion represents the individual in and for itself or I's coming back to itself as U (synthesis) which includes the first two though elevated to a higher level. The conclusion represents the idea or thesis as having returned to itself by dint of its having gone out of itself in its self-particularization in the minor premise. Since he regards this linking of individual and universal by a mediating particular as the core of the syllogism and since he holds that everything is a particular which joins the individual and the universal, Hegel construes the syllogistic form as the form of all things.

Finally, a similar but different dialectic characterizes Aquinas' idea of the syllogism. By its joining the S and P terms in the conclusion, the middle term is the means by which the one-sided wide generality of the P term in the major premise (rule) and the opposite one-sided narrow particularity of the minor premise (case) are both overcome in the conclusion which is the result of both rule and case. There the two are joined in a synthesis which gives new knowledge. The one-sided wide generality of the P term in the major premise is mitigated by its being linked in the conclusion to an opposite particular, i.e. the S term. By the same token, the one-sided narrow particularity of the S term in the minor premise is overcome by its being joined in the conclusion with an opposite generality, i.e. the P term. P's being linked to S tempers and corrects its relatively one-sided generality in the major premise. In so doing it both retains and uplifts P. For P figures in the new knowledge expressed in the conclusion. By the same token, S's being linked to P in the same conclusion tempers and corrects its relatively one-sided particularity in the minor premise. And once again this preserves S and yet uplifts it due to S's participation in the new knowledge of the conclusion. The result (the conclusion) thus represents a synthesis of universal and particular which constitutes a more recondite knowledge caused by the more direct or easier known premises. In this dialectic, the thesis is the one-sided generality of P in the major premise, the antithesis is the one-sided individuality of S in the minor premise, and the synthesis is the union of both in the conclusion on a higher plain in the sense specified. To use C. S. Peirce's characterization of the syllogism as proceeding from rule and case to result, the general rule (major premise) is one-sided generality and can be taken as thesis. By contrast, the case (minor premise) is one-sided particularity and can be taken as antithesis. Finally, the result of rule and case which is the conclusion counterbalances the one-sidedness of both rule and case by combining elements of each one (i.e. S and P).[204] To the extent that it does, this new knowledge in the conclusion can be taken as being a synthesis of the rule and the case and hence a higher type of knowledge than either one.

---

[204] Though Peirce conceded that his own pragmaticism was "closely related to the Hegelian absolute idealism" (*Collected Papers of Charles Sanders Peirce*, 5.436, 231), one cannot infer from this that he endorsed the Hegelian dialectical account of the syllogism.

Index

abstraction
    formal vs. total, 68–69
    vs. precision, 80–81
Aristotle, 9, 10–11, 26, 72, 76, 109–110, 111–112, 117, 121–122
Averroes, 128
belief, 52ff
    sense and referent of, 54
Berkeley, George, 62
Bolzano, B., 71
Bradley, F.H., 65–66
category mistake, 49
causal reciprocity, 8–9
Chisholm, R.M., 47n
classes, 79-80
conceptualism, 88–89
correspondence theory, 48
Descartes, 86
dialectic
    in Aquinas, 116–130
    in Hegel, 107–116
Donagan, A., 63-64
Edwards, Jonathan, 39n
efficient cause
    dilemma of, 2–3
    subsidiary and basic, 5–8
    types of, 1-2
epiphenomenalism, 86–87
existential neutrality, 71, 72, 75
Fichte, J. G. 109
final cause, 1, 7–9, 20–21. *See also* teleology
    dilemma of, 10
    external vs. internal, 44
Gadamer, Hans-Georg, 106
Gilson, E., 63,64n.
Hegel, G.W.F., 105, ff
    and dialectic, 107ff
    and the syllogism, 114ff
hylomorphism, 78, 85, 91
idealism, 62, 83
identity materialism, 82–83
identity-thesis, 54
immanent activity, 35

vs. transeunt activity, 37

James, William, 71

judgment

   as analysis and synthesis, 79

   in Hegel's dialectic, 113

 related to sensation and apprehension, 116ff

Kant, I., 89, 108

knowledge, 52ff

   sense and reference in, 55ff

   vs. true belief, 59–60

Leibniz, 33

Locke, John, 62

mentalism, 45–46

Meinong, A., 70

mind-body issue, 77ff

moderate realism, 67, 76

Moore, G.E., 63, 74

Mure, G.R.G., 106, 109

nominalism, 88, 90

Ockham's Razor, 18

one-truth theory, 13

Peirce, C.S., 28

   and teleology, 28, 43

Plato, 61, 63

pragmatism, 43

predicables, 79ff

   and dualism, 85

   and idealism, 83–84

   and identity materialism, 83

predication, 69–76

proposition-theorists, 46ff

Quine, W.V., 50, 65

realism

   Aquinas's, 70ff

   moderate, 67, 76

   robust, 63–64

   senses of, 62ff

realist principle, 61

regress

   Bradley's, 66

   Ryle's, 65

   third man, 65, 76

Russell, B., 61, 66–67, 74

Saint Anselm, 18, 21

Saint Thomas Aquinas

   on immanent activity, 35

   on predication, 69–74

    on the soul, 91ff

    on the syllogism, 126ff

    on turning to the phantasms, 117–118

Sartre, J.P., 46

Schelling, F. W. J., 109

sentence-tokens, 45, 61

simple apprehension, 14–15

skepticism, 54

soul, 91ff

    as form of the body, 98ff

    as immaterial, 92ff

Stace, W.T., 106, 114

Stallknecht, N.P., 89

Taylor, Charles, 107

teleology *see also* final cause

    and reasoning, 29–35

    and truth, 12ff

    in things, 8–11

transeunt activity, 37

truth

    as assimilated to mind, 14

    as known, 23–24

    bearer of, 45ff

    conceptual, 22

    definition of, 14, 19

    practical and theoretical, 12

universals, 61, 74

    problem of, 63–64

Veatch, H. B., 75n

William of Champeaux, 63, 74

Wittgenstein, L., 73n, 84n

www.ingramcontent.com/pod-product-compliance
Lightning Source LLC
Chambersburg PA
CBHW020949230426

43666CB00005B/247